HOME MAINTENANCE
MADE EASY

WHAT TO DO,
WHEN TO DO IT,
WHEN TO CALL
FOR HELP

MyHome Press

Home Maintenance Made Easy: What to Do, When to Do It, When to Call for Help

MyHome Press, a Service of the National Association of Home Builders

Elizabeth M. Rich	Director, Book Publishing
Natalie C. Holmes	Book Editor
Cruzial Design	Cover Design
pixiedesign	Composition
McNaughton & Gunn	Printing
Gerald M. Howard	NAHB Chief Executive Officer
Mark Pursell	NAHB Senior Vice President, Exhibitions, Marketing & Sales
Lakisha Campbell, CAE	NAHB Vice President, Publishing & Affinity Programs

Disclaimer

This publication provides accurate information on the subject matter covered. The publisher is selling it with the understanding that the publisher is not providing legal, accounting, or other professional service. If you need legal advice or other expert assistance, obtain the services of a qualified professional experienced in the subject matter involved. Reference herein to any specific commercial products, process, or service by trade name, trademark, manufacturer, or otherwise does not necessarily constitute or imply its endorsement, recommendation, or favored status by the National Association of Home Builders. The views and opinions of the author expressed in this publication do not necessarily state or reflect those of the National Association of Home Builders, and they shall not be used to advertise or endorse a product.

Printed in the United States of America

16 15 14 13   1 2 3 4 5

Library of Congress Cataloging-in-Publication Data

Home maintenance made easy : what to do, when to do it, when to call for help / [National Association of Home Builders].
     pages cm
  Includes index.
  ISBN 978-0-86718-718-2 (alkaline paper) -- ISBN 978-0-86718-719-9 1. Dwellings--Maintenance and repair--Amateurs'
manuals. I. National Association of Home Builders (U.S.)
  TH4817.3.H6475 2013
  643'.7--dc23
                          2013009418

For further information, please contact:

National Association of Home Builders
1201 15th Street, NW
Washington, DC 20005-2800
800-223-2665

myhomepress.com

CONTENTS

ACKNOWLEDGMENTS

My Home Press is grateful to Bill Asdal, Ted Clifton, Alan Hanbury, Michael LeCorgne, and Allen Schuler for their professional insights in anticipating and answering the questions that are important to home owners like you.

INTRODUCTION

Buying and owning a home is an exhilarating and energizing experience—sort of like falling in love and getting married. The home catches your eye and captures your attention; you picture what it would be like living there; you draw up a plan to make it your own. The opportunity to create your personal living space, raise a family, participate in the local community, and even build long-term wealth is why homeownership is the ultimate "American Dream." But without proper care your home may look and feel neglected and the once-promising romance can suffer.

So although décor (think wedding planning) is probably what captivates you when you begin the romance with your new home, keep in mind that what will ensure its longevity is not the window dressing—paper, paint, and finishes—you picture in your fantasy. They will change over time with your tastes and home fashion. Regular maintenance, on the other hand, is the glue that will keep your home together and functioning well for you and your family for many years.

When you purchase a new home, you have the benefit of the builder and others intimately familiar with its construction to explain the home's systems, components, maintenance, and warranty. If you purchase a used home, the seller may provide a warranty as a purchase incentive. The sales agent may be able to point out the home's major modifications or improvements. But he or she probably won't know much about the details behind the façade. Likewise, learning the requirements for operating or maintaining the home's major and minor systems and components will be up to you. In either case, new or used home, you—the blissful home owner in love with your new space—are responsible for its day-to-day upkeep.

How well you maintain your home's *building envelope*, major and minor functional systems, and items that the next owners (if you sell) may want to keep, such as flooring, cabinetry, and bathroom components and

fixtures, will determine your home's *effective age* and impact its longevity and market value if you or your heirs decide to sell it. Learn the simple measures you can take regularly to preserve your home's value. Save money and avoid disasters by calling on professionals such as carpenters, plumbers, electricians, and painters as needed to maintain and improve your home.

This book explains the small but significant steps you can and should take to keep your home in good working order and maintain its value. It provides a place to store important papers (receipts, instructions, warranties, contact information) related to your home. It includes places to write quick notes, such as contact information, dates, and reminders. The book also includes monthly suggestions for maintenance and cleaning that will simplify upkeep and ensure your responsibilities as a home owner are manageable. After all, a home is not only the place where you spend most of your time, it is also the single largest investment most people will make in their lifetime.

 TIP

> You can go to **www.nahb.org/hmme** to download PDF forms where you can store comprehensive contact information, maintenance records, and other details about your home, including paint colors, electronically.

This manual was designed to help you

- understand the components of your home;
- care for and maintain your home; and
- organize important records about your home.

Although your home includes more than 3,000 component parts produced and installed by thousands of people, you can ensure its durability and living pleasure just by understanding a few basics of maintenance and home improvement.

SAFETY AND SECURITY

To keep your family safe and secure, practice fire prevention and maintain your smoke detectors, carbon monoxide detectors, and security systems. In addition, you can use the Checklist for Extended Absence on page 76 and at **www.nahb.org/hmme** to prepare to lock and leave your home when you need to travel.

FIRE PREVENTION

All family members should understand fire prevention and fire danger.

Train Family Members

- Ensure that all family members know the escape routes to use in a fire.
- Conduct regular fire drills.
- Test your smoke detectors to ensure they function and so everyone will recognize the warning alarm's sound. Follow the manufacturer's directions for cleaning and servicing your smoke detectors.
- Teach children how and why to dial 911.
- Have a general-use fire extinguisher and ensure all family members know where it is and how to use it.
- Teach children how to use appliances, such as irons, gas ranges, and toasters, safely.

Prevent Fires

- Store matches away from children and heat sources.
- Don't smoke in bed.
- Don't leave small children home alone, even for a short time.
- Maintain appliances in clean and safe working condition.
- Don't overload electrical outlets.
- Make sure all electrical cords are in good repair.
- Use properly sized fuses.

FIRE EXTINGUISHER

Every home owner should buy at least one fire extinguisher. Each member of the family should know where it is and how and when to use it.

Fires from combustible solids such as wood, cloth, or paper differ from electrical and chemical fires. Most home supply centers sell multipurpose fire extinguishers you can use for most types of small fires.

 CAUTION

If you are not sure what type of fire extinguisher you have, do not use it on an electrical or grease fire.

- Don't place flammable objects or materials near the stove.
- Keep the range hood filter clean to prevent grease buildup.
- Allow space for cooling around electrical equipment.
- Unplug the iron after use. Do not leave an iron that is on unattended.
- Use electric blankets with care, following manufacturer directions.
- Store volatile materials (paint, gasoline for the lawn mower, and so on) in appropriate containers, away from flames (such as pilot lights) or heat sources, ideally in a garage or building that is not part of your habitable space. Many trash collection services offer disposal of hazardous items. Check your community's resources.
- Keep flammable objects and materials away from the barbeque grill.
- Follow directions for using your gas fireplace. Do not leave the fireplace unattended when it is on.

TIP

Keep a home first aid kit or first aid materials in a convenient location. Buy and keep with it a booklet on first aid and home safety.

- Use the proper screen or glass with your fireplace
- During holidays, ensure that all cords and connections are in good condition and of appropriate capacity for electrical decorations. Do not run cords under mats or areas where they can be stepped on.
- If you decide to remodel, finish the basement, or add onto your home, obtain a building permit and work with trained professionals. Ensure that all building department inspections occur and that the work complies with all applicable codes. This also applies to installing a gas line for an outdoor barbeque, a gas fireplace, a clothes dryer, or other gas appliance.

If you have a wood-burning fireplace:

- Arrange for professional inspection and cleaning of the fireplace or chimney no less than once every 2 years if you use the fireplace frequently. Oil burners, wood, and other combustion fireplaces create creosote and other unburned materials that can stick to the sides of *flues*. During intense fires these materials can reignite and damage the flue or even start a house fire. The inspector should check the brick and mortar for cracks/damage. If there are problems, hire a professional to fix them.
- Inspect flues quarterly.
- Maintain the *spark arrester* on the chimney.
- Never use liquid fire starters (such as for a charcoal barbeque) in an indoor fireplace.
- Use a screen or glass doors when a fire is burning (but don't close the glass doors over a roaring fire).
- Confirm the fire is out before closing the flue.
- Do not leave the fireplace unattended while a fire is burning.[1]

Read more about fire prevention in chapter 6, Electrical Systems and chapter 7, Fireplaces.

CARBON MONOXIDE DETECTORS, SECURITY SYSTEMS, SMOKE DETECTORS

Depending on your home's age, the following safety features may have been included in construction or they may be retrofits to an existing home. If you have them, maintain them; if you don't, you may want to consider adding them.

Carbon Monoxide Detectors

Your home may be equipped with one or more carbon monoxide detectors. These devices resemble smoke detectors. They are designed to sound an alarm if carbon monoxide in the home reaches a harmful level. Carefully review the manufacturer's instructions for the care and maintenance of your carbon monoxide detector(s). Some units are battery operated and some are wired into your home's electrical system. Either type should be tested frequently. If the alarm on your carbon monoxide detector sounds, treat it as you would a smoke alarm: evacuate the house immediately and call the fire department.

Security Systems

Although security systems are installed to work autonomously, you should regularly (a) check that the alarm and circuits are in working order and (b) inspect sensors one by one (consult your instruction manual). **Check primary and backup batteries once a month, and replace them at least once a year or according to the manufacturer's recommendation.**

Smoke Detectors

Smoke detectors are either battery operated or connected to your home's electrical system. If a smoke detector chirps, the battery needs replacement. Most use a 9-volt battery. Carefully review the manufacturer's literature to familiarize yourself with each unit. When they are set off, most battery-operated detectors will continue to sound until a reset button is pushed. Other types will stop automatically when smoke is cleared from the chamber. Check the manufacturer's literature to see which type you have so you may act accordingly if the detector is accidentally triggered. Periodically test the detector to see if it is working properly.

Different types of detectors will require different care. Follow the manufacturer's recommendations for periodic maintenance. Maintenance may include replacing the lightbulbs, replacing the batteries, vacuuming the unit inside and out, and cleaning it with a cotton swab and alcohol.

LOCKS

If added home security is a concern, consider these items before installing additional locks to your doors:

- Locks should be located so they cannot be reached by breaking a small windowpane in or near the door.
- Locks that require a key on the inside are potentially dangerous if an emergency occurs. When this type of lock is used, be sure a spare key is always handy to prevent trapping anyone inside the house.
- Chains or locks will be most secure if the screws and bolts used to attach them go all the way through the door or frame and cannot be removed from the outside.
- A metal insulated door may require the services of an expert to install new locks properly.

 REMINDERS

- Check fire extinguisher annually to ensure the charge is still in the green area of the scale. If needed, you can have it recharged at a specialty store. A qualified and licensed professional should recharge it.
- Inspect flues quarterly and arrange for professional inspection and cleaning at least every 2 years if you use the fireplace frequently.
- Check carbon monoxide detectors monthly.
- Change smoke detector batteries in the spring and fall when you change your clocks. Check them quarterly.

Hazardous Waste Disposal

_____

Call for Pickup

_____

Phone Number for Hazardous Waste Facility

_____

URL for Hazardous Waste Facility

_____

Days/Hours for Dropoff

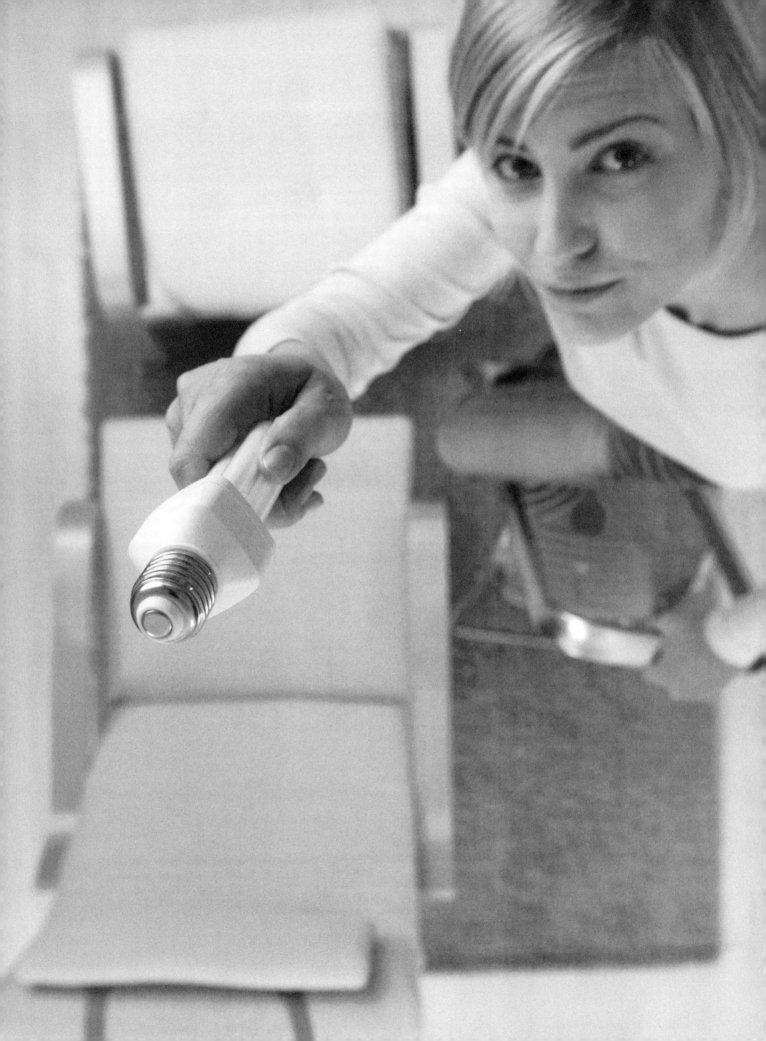

REDUCING UTILITY BILLS

Your household's lifestyle is the most significant variable affecting your utility bills. Identical homes on the same street may have utility bills that vary by 100%. By living smarter in your home, you can maximize the benefits of insulation and other energy-efficient features.

COOLING COSTS

Open doors, windows, and fireplace flues can negate the positive effects of insulation. Clogged air filters can block cooling air. To save energy and keep your home more comfortable in warm months, keep windows and doors closed, run heat-generating appliances such as dishwashers or conventional ovens later in the evening, and set your thermostat to a higher temperature at night. Remember that in the summer, part of the heat removed from the home by the cooling system is generated inside by lights, appliances, and people.

Use these common-sense measures to save energy and money:

- Close the windows and doors when the heating/cooling system is working.
- Don't run the dryer, stove, or oven on a hot summer day.
- Adjust thermostat settings to 68°F or lower in the winter and 75°F or higher in the summer.
- Open drapes or blinds on the sunny side of the house during winter days to take advantage of *passive solar heating*. Remember to close them as the sun sets.
- Close drapes, blinds, or curtains on hot summer days when the sun shines into your home.
- Use a programmable thermostat (as applicable for your system) to keep your house comfortably warm in the winter and comfortably cool in the summer. Use the day/night settings and weekday/weekend settings.

- Never turn the heat off in winter—even during an extended vacation. If you do, you may come home and find a frozen or burst pipe.
- Avoid setting your thermostat at a colder setting than normal when you turn on your air conditioner. It will not cool your home any faster but it may result in excessive cooling and unnecessary expense.
- Use *compact fluorescent light (CFL)* bulbs with the ENERGY STAR® label.
- Replace filters on furnaces according to filter manufacturers' instructions. A clogged filter will reduce air flow, making the air *handler* work harder and possibly causing it to fail prematurely.
- Clean warm-air *registers*, baseboard heaters, and radiators as needed with a wand attachment on your vacuum. The idea is to make the flow of air, either forced or by convection, as easy as can be. Pet hair, dander, cobwebs, and dust can block openings.

- Don't block registers or air *returns* with furniture, carpeting, or drapes.
- Air-dry dishes instead of using the dishwasher drying cycle.
- Use cold water to operate a garbage disposal.
- When baking, begin using the oven no more than five minutes after you have preheated it. Turn it off a few minutes before reaching the required baking time.
- Turn off electric burners a few minutes before cooking is complete.
- Instead of using your regular oven or range during hot weather, microwave or use the grill.
- Turn off your computer and monitor when you are not using them.
- Plug home electronics, such as TVs and DVD players, into power strips; turn the power strips off when the equipment is not in use (TVs and DVDs in standby mode still use several watts of power).

- Place an insulation jacket on the water heater.
- If your dishwasher has a hot-water booster, lower the thermostat on your water heater to 120°F. This not only reduces energy use, it can help prevent scalding.
- Wash only full loads of dishes and clothes. This is easier to do with new ENERGY STAR® appliances with variable load cycles.
- Look for the ENERGY STAR® label on home appliances and products. ENERGY STAR® products meet strict efficiency guidelines set by the U.S. Department of Energy and the EPA.

- Turn off kitchen, bath, and other exhaust fans within 20 minutes of finishing cooking or bathing. When replacing exhaust fans, consider installing high-efficiency, low-noise models. Add timers at the switches.
- During the heating season, keep the window coverings on your south-facing windows open during the day to allow the sunlight to enter your home and closed at night to reduce the chill you may feel from cold windows.
- Keep all south-facing glass clean.
- Make sure objects do not block the sunlight shining on concrete slab floors or heat-absorbing walls.
- Avoid placing lamps, televisions, or other heat sources near your thermostat(s). A thermostat senses the heat, which may cause air-conditioning to operate more than necessary.

COMPACT FLUORESCENT LIGHTING (CFL)

One of the greatest energy savers is CFLs. These miniature versions of full-size fluorescent lights use an arc discharge through a phosphor-lined tube instead of heating a resistance filament as in incandescent light bulbs. A CFL consists of a lamp, lamp holder, and ballast. The ballast provides the electrical control to strike and maintain the arc. Although fluorescent lighting previously would cast a bluish hue, the color quality of newer compact fluorescent lighting is almost indistinguishable from incandescent lighting. You can purchase CFLs in various color temperatures from warm to cool. Some CFLs even mimic daylight.

The average rated life of a CFL is 8–15 times that of incandescent lights. CFLs typically have a rated lifespan of 6,000–15,000 hours, whereas incandescent lamps are usually manufactured to have a lifespan of 750 hours or 1,000 hours. A 23–30-watt CFL has approximately the same light output as a 100-watt incandescent bulb.

To optimize the value of CFLs, use them in areas that are lit for relatively extended periods of time (15 minutes or longer), such as outdoors, and in the kitchen, family room, and bedrooms. Switching a CFL on and off too frequently will shorten its life. CFLs contain small amounts of mercury, so take them to a qualified disposal facility rather than placing them in the garbage where the mercury could seep into a landfill.

 REMINDERS

- Clean or replace filters every 1–3 months or as the manufacturer recommends.
- Clean/replace kitchen exhaust fan filters quarterly. Clean refrigerator coils annually.

NOTES:

Managing moisture in and around your home is one of the most important things you can do to ensure its longevity, make it comfortable to live in, and prevent damage to its contents.

HIGH PERFORMANCE HOME BENEFITS

New high performance homes incorporate the latest building science principles to control temperature and humidity, maintain indoor air quality (IAQ), and increase energy efficiency. Although your home may not include all of the latest air-sealing, ventilation, and moisture-management technology, you will be more comfortable in your home and it will last longer if you do everything possible to manage moisture. This includes replacing filters, controlling humidity, and when outside air is cool and dry, allowing fresh air into your home.

RELATIVE HUMIDITY

Relative humidity is the amount of water the air contains compared with the amount it could contain at a specific temperature. When the relative humidity is 100%, the air is retaining the most moisture possible without precipitation. You will feel most comfortable in your home when relative humidity is 30%–60%.

When relative humidity falls below 30%, nasal passages dry out and you get stuffed up. Your skin feels itchy and is susceptible to cracking. Eyes become irritated, especially for contact lens wearers. As relative humidity approaches 20%, static electricity and *ozone* increase. Wood furniture and floors shrink and crack. Asthma and allergies flare up. Less moisture makes the air feel cooler, so occupants turn up the heat. Utility bills go up.

Conversely, when the level is above 60%, the air is too wet, which is also harmful to both the home and the home owners. Excess humidity can breed mold, pests, and rot. Too-humid air is more likely to cause heatstroke, heat exhaustion, headaches, and dehydration than less humid air.

Keeping indoor humidity in the commonly-recommended range of 30%–60% (as well as introducing fresh air into the home) can improve indoor environmental quality. Your kitchen, bathrooms, and laundry room—all areas that generate excessive moisture—may have exhaust fans. Use these fans to eliminate excess moisture and odors. Clean them at least every 5 years (for those that don't need lubrication), and yearly for those that do. Check for dust and lint buildup around the dampers, blades, and intact grille.

A whole-house dehumidification system (or an AC unit capable of stand-alone dehumidification) may have been integrated into your home. To function properly, the system will require occasional cleaning to remove accumulated mineral deposits. Some systems have an evaporative pad which may need to be replaced periodically. Follow the manufacturer's instructions.

BASEMENTS

As with all the other parts of your house, basement walls are not waterproof, and a perfectly dry basement may have wet walls during the summer because of *condensation* that forms when warm moist air hits a cold surface. Where conditions warrant it, builders dampproof the underground portions of the foundation to prevent water entering from surrounding soil.

How to repair basement leaks depends upon local conditions. Each case is different. Before making expensive structural repairs to correct wet wall conditions, thoroughly check your drainage system. Repairing or adjusting downspouts or gutters will help to carry surface water away from foundation walls. Ideally, the downspout will end 6'–10' from the house. Slope soil and gardens away from the structure by 6" over that distance.

If the ground outside your basement slopes toward the wall, pack and bank up soil so water will drain away. Avoid planting shrubbery within less than 3' of the foundation. Never water your plants toward the foundation.

 TIP

Condensation occurs wherever relatively warm moist air inside a home makes contact with a colder surface—a window, a basement wall, an exposed pipe.

MILDEW

Even in climate-controlled homes, mildew (another name for mold) can appear in areas of high humidity, such as bathrooms and laundry rooms. You can take positive steps to reduce or eliminate mold growth by lowering humidity.

Vent clothes dryers to the outdoors. Ventilate rooms, particularly kitchens and bathrooms, by opening the windows, using exhaust fans, or running the air conditioner or a dehumidifier to remove excess moisture in the air. Promptly clean up spills, condensation, and other sources of moisture. Thoroughly dry any wet surfaces or material. Do not let piles of wet towels or clothing stand in the home.

Regular vacuuming and cleaning will also help reduce spore levels. If you notice mold or mildew developing, depending on the surface, you can scrub the affected area with a commercial mixture of trisodium phosphate (TSP) or a commercial cleaner like Jomax and bleach. Always test cleanser on a small inconspicuous spot. Read more about moisture management in Plumbing, chapter 5, and the sections on Roofs, Gutters, and Downspouts of chapter 12, Exterior.

REMINDERS

- Clean bathroom/laundry room exhaust fans every 1 to 5 years. Check for dust and lint that accumulate around dampers, blades, and grille.
- Check basements and crawl spaces quarterly for unusual dampness, leaks, and evidence of termites or other infestation.

NOTES:

4 HEATING, VENTILATION, AND AIR-CONDITIONING (HVAC)

Your central air-conditioning system can provide years of reliable comfort if you properly maintain it. It should be able to hold a temperature of 78°F (measured in the center of each room at a height of 5') or a variance of 15 degrees from the outdoor temperature. The *compressor* must be level to operate correctly.

Among the other components of your HVAC system are a mechanism to filter incoming outdoor air, registers to deliver conditioned air to individual rooms, and returns that allow air to reenter the handler that heats or cools and recirculates air. Your system also may include a humidifier, separate ventilation to allow or push fresh outside air into your home, or both.

ANNUAL INSPECTION

Have your HVAC system checked and cleaned periodically by a professional. Test your furnace in early fall and your air-conditioning in early spring when temperatures are moderate. If there are problems, it's much better to discover them before extreme temperatures set in. See your system's instruction manual for suggested frequency, but have it checked at least once every two years.

Before you turn the air-conditioner on for the season, ensure that the condensate drain is free of clogs. Professionals handle this in a number of ways—by pouring a quart of water or a cup of bleach into, or in some cases blowing air through, the line. A clogged line may go unnoticed at first but can cause a great deal of damage if the drain overflows as a result.

SYSTEM COMPONENTS

Your HVAC system includes the unit itself, which may have a fuse above the on-off switch, or a pilot, and a filter or multiple filters, ductwork, registers, and air returns.

HIGH PERFORMANCE HOMES

Although conventional wisdom promoted allowing buildings to "breathe," modern building science has proven that natural air leakage is unreliable, can compromise building durability, and increases energy consumption. Instead of allowing homes to breathe, builders of high performance or *green homes* prevent air infiltration by using air barriers. These materials prevent air movement between unconditioned and conditioned space and control fresh air exchange via mechanical ventilation. Tight construction and consistent, controlled, fresh air ventilation (and removal of pollutants at their source through spot ventilation) are essential for green buildings built according to the newest codes.

Registers

The registers throughout your home help to regulate the flow of air and maintain the desired temperature. By opening and closing the registers and dampers, you can control how much air enters a room. Carefully adjusted dampers will work with the thermostat to maintain the temperature of your home. Generally, you can reduce the heat in seldom-used or interior rooms. However, if you shut off heat to a room that contains pipes for a hot-water baseboard heating system in a climate where freezing is possible, you risk allowing water in the pipes to freeze. If you have a combined cooling and heating system, the same registers and dampers will be used to regulate the flow of the hot and cold air to the rooms. Registers and returns should never be obstructed by furniture, drapes, or other objects. Your HVAC system is designed to operate most efficiently by using all available registers and returns.

Ducts

Depending on its location, your furnace may have a *combustion air* duct. Never cover or block this duct: your furnace needs outside air to supply sufficient oxygen. If you block the combustion air intake, the system has to pull combustion air from elsewhere, like the conditioned part of your home or from fireplace flues. This creates a carbon monoxide poisoning risk. The combustion air duct is functioning normally if it allows cold air in.

Also, consider the facts before you buy into professional duct cleaning services. A U.S. Environmental Protection Agency (EPA) study found no proof that duct cleaning improves indoor air quality or prevents health problems.

Filters

Most central HVAC systems have an air filter. The instruction manual for your system will tell you the type of filter to use and how to clean or replace it. Many forced-air systems have air filters, usually found near where the conditioned air returns from other rooms. These filters remove dirt and dust from the air. For efficiency, they should be cleaned or replaced once a month whenever your system is being used. If you cannot see through the filter held up to a light, it needs to be changed. Usually,

replacement involves removing one or two metal screws, pulling out the dirty filter, and inserting a new one.

Other systems have latches or dual stacked filters. Use only water to clean permanent washable removable filters. Tap or air dry and leave the unit off briefly after cleaning the filter. Some systems may have electronic air filtering systems. Read the instruction manual for your system for specific directions. *Radiant* heating and *hydronic* baseboard systems do not have filters.

> ### INDOOR AIR
> Today's energy efficient homes are built to provide maximum comfort at minimum utility costs for the home owner. Energy-efficient design, however, results in tighter homes with a slower rate of air exchange than older homes. Cigarette smoke, pets, materials used in furniture or carpet, and other factors may affect the quality of the air in your home. Follow manufacturers' instructions and regularly change the air filter in your HVAC system, according to the schedule in your manual or at least every three months during the heating season.

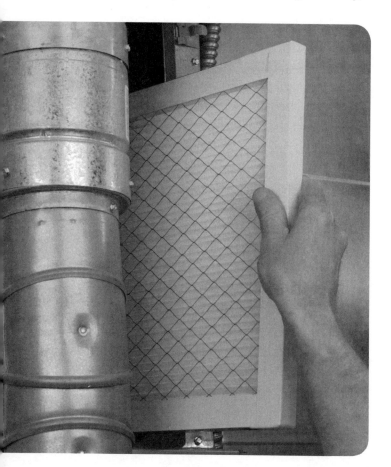

Fuses

If your furnace has a fuse (above the on-off switch) to absorb spikes in the line such as close lightning strikes or power surges, keep extra fuses on hand. The fuse has a spring that depresses when the fuse is tripped.

On-Off Switch

This switch looks like a light switch. In the "off" position, it shuts down the blower and overrides all furnace commands. It is usually only turned off for maintenance.

Pilot

To light a manually lit pilot on a furnace, follow these steps:

1. Remove the cover panel to expose the pilot.
2. Rotate the "on-off" pilot knob to "pilot."
3. Depress and hold the red button while holding a match to the pilot.

4. Continue to press the button for 30 to 60 seconds. *(When you release it, the pilot should stay lit; if it doesn't, follow step 5)*

5. Wait several minutes to allow the gas to dissipate; repeat steps 1–4.

Note: Instructions should be on or near the unit.

TROUBLESHOOTING: NO HEAT

Before you call for service, check these items:

- Thermostat is set to "heat" and temperature is set above the room temperature.
- Blower panel cover is installed correctly for the furnace blower (fan) to operate. Similar to a clothes dryer door, this panel presses a button that allows the fan motor to come on. If the button is not pushed, the furnace will not operate.
- Breaker on the main electrical panel is on. (If a breaker trips, you must flip it from the tripped position to the off position before you can turn it back on.)
- Switch on the side of the furnace is on.
- Furnace fuse is good. (See manufacturer literature for size and location.)

- Gas line is open at the main meter and at the side of the furnace.
- Filter is clean to allow airflow.
- Registers are open.
- Air returns are unobstructed.

Even if troubleshooting does not identify a solution, the information you gather will be useful to the service provider you call.[2]

TROUBLESHOOTING: NO AIR-CONDITIONING

Before you call for service, check these items:

- Thermostat is set to "cool" and the temperature is set below the room temperature.
- Blower panel cover is installed correctly for the furnace blower (fan) to operate (see Troubleshooting: No Heat section).
- Air conditioner and furnace breakers on the main electrical panel are on. (If a breaker trips, you must flip it from the tripped position to the off position before you can turn it back on.)
- The disconnect switch on the outside wall near the air conditioner is on. (It should only be turned off while the unit is being serviced.)
- Switch on the side of the furnace is on.
- Fuse in furnace is good (see manufacturer literature for size and location).
- Filter is clean to allow air flow.
- Registers are open.
- Air returns are unobstructed.

ODOR AND NOISE

Your system may emit an odor for a few minutes after it is turned on if it is new or if it has not been used for an extended time period. The smell is from dust that settles in the ducts and it should dissipate quickly. Also, metal ductwork typically will tick or pop. However *oil canning*, which distorts the duct and makes a very loud noise, is considered extreme and should be corrected.

Even if troubleshooting does not identify a solution, the information you gather will be useful to the service provider you call.[3]

EVAPORATIVE COOLING

An *evaporative cooler* is an efficient way to cool a home in a dry climate. The system draws air across wet pads and circulates cool moist air into the home. Maintain the system as follows:

- Check connections and distribution lines twice a year for obstructions or leaks.
- Drain the reservoir and replace the water monthly.
- Replace the pads once a year.

HEAT PUMP

Instead of a separate furnace and air conditioner, your home may have a *heat pump* for winter heating and summer cooling. During the colder months, heat pumps work by drawing on the small amount of heat present in the air (or in the ground in the case of ground-source heat pumps) to heat the home. In the summer, heat pumps reverse this process and cool the air in the house by drawing heat outside.

Most heat pump systems use auxiliary electric heating elements to supply additional heat when outside temperatures are too low to draw sufficient heat to keep the house warm (typically below about 30°F). If the light indicating the auxiliary unit stays on when the outside temperature is higher than 30°F, call for service.

Keeping the thermostat at a constant setting limits the use of this backup system and will help keep utility bills down. Do not expect dramatic temperature differences at the air vents as with other kinds of systems. Although the vents will not feel hot, the air discharged is warmer than the room air by as much as 20°. Avoid manually setting back the thermostat unless you plan to keep the house at a lower temperature for a fairly long period, such as over a weekend when you will be away. Also, unless you have a setback thermostat designed to work with a heat pump system, do not turn the thermostat down in the evenings.

To adjust rooms for comfort during heating season in a home that uses a heat pump, never close off more than one supply register at a time. Instead, find a permanent thermostat setting that will keep all rooms comfortable by following these steps:

- Open all vents.
- Gradually adjust the thermostat (a half degree at a time) until the coolest room is comfortable.
- Close vents in the warmer rooms until all rooms are comfortable.

Reverse the process during cooling season. Follow the manufacturer's instructions on changing air filters and other routine maintenance

 TIP

Place outlet covers (plastic plugs) in unused electrical outlets, which can emit cold outside air.

TROUBLESHOOTING: *NO HEAT OR AUXILIARY HEAT STAYS ON*

When you have no heat or the auxiliary heater stays on when the outside temperature is at least 30°F, check the following before calling for service:

- Thermostat is set to "heat" and temperature is set above the room temperature.
- Breaker on the main electrical panel is on.
- Filter is clean.
- Vents in individual rooms are open.
- Air returns are unobstructed.
- Outside unit is not blocked by snow or other obstructions.
- Outside coil does not have excessive ice buildup. (Frost may accumulate on the coils when the outside temperature is below freezing. The system will defrost automatically for up to 10 minutes as often as every 90 minutes. Temperatures in the home will be lower during the defrost cycle.)

Even if the preceding steps do not identify a solution, the information you gather will be useful to your service provider.[4]

HOT WATER HEATING SYSTEM

With a hot water system, sometimes called a hydronic system, water is heated to about 180°F by an oil- or gas-fired boiler and distributed through pipes by a small pump called a circulator. The two most common types of hot water heating systems are *radiant* and *hot water baseboard (HWBB)*. In radiant systems, the hot water pipes may be in the ceiling, walls, or floors.

In HWBB systems, the hot water runs through copper pipes behind baseboard panels with openings in the top and bottom to allow the cold air to enter, pass over a set of aluminum fins, and rise when it is warmed. Some manufacturers make the two types of heating panels in matching units so they can be interlocked and used together. With radiant electric heat, electric heating elements provide the source of radiation. Both types of baseboard heating units should be vacuumed periodically to remove hair, spider webs, or other contaminants that obstruct air movement through the aluminum fins that transfer the heat. Also ensure the area under the baseboard enclosures is not blocked by rugs that have curled up, toys, or other items, and that furniture is not placed too close to the units.

 REMINDERS

- Have your HVAC system serviced in the early spring and early fall.
- Clean or replace filters as needed every 1–3 months or as the manufacturer recommends.

5 PLUMBING

Knowing how to maintain your plumbing fixtures, when to attempt a repair yourself, and when you must call in a professional are the keys to preventing leaks, back-ups, and potential water damage to your home.

INTAKE VALVES

All members of your household should know where the water intake valves are for your plumbing system and how to open and close them. Label each one with a shipping or luggage tag. You will rarely need to use them, but in an emergency or if you need to make minor repairs, they will be easy to locate. Intake valves for toilets are usually under the water chamber. Those for sinks are usually under the sink, while the main intake valve is usually near the point where the water enters the house.

TROUBLESHOOTING: NO WATER

Confirm:

- Main shutoff is open.
- Individual shutoffs for each water-using fixture are open.

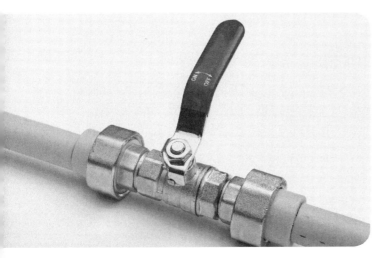

WATER HEATER

Set your water heater to 120° (the "hot" setting on an electric water heater and "normal" on a gas water heater) if your dishwasher has a booster water heater. If not, set your water heater temperature to 140° (the "B" or high setting on an electric water heater). On gas heaters be sure the air intake is not obstructed. Avoid storing anything near the water heater that might obstruct the flow of air or create a fire hazard. Water heaters normally collect small quantities of scale and dirty water. They require cleaning as follows:

- Shut the water intake valve and turn off the power source for your water heater. (Failure to turn off the power source could cause the heating element to burn out.)
- Open the valve at the bottom of the heater and completely drain the tank.
- Open the water intake valve and allow some water to flow through to flush out the remaining sediment.
- Shut the valve at the bottom of the tank.

When the tank is full, follow the manufacturer's instructions for restoring heat. Never light a pilot on an empty gas water heater and always turn off the gas before shutting off the cold water supply to the tank. Follow the same procedure in lighting your water heater pilot as used for a gas furnace pilot.

TROUBLESHOOTING: NO HOT WATER

Before calling for service, confirm:

- Pilot is lit.
- Temperature setting is not on "vacation" or set too low.
- Water supply valve is open.

Check the temperature and pressure relief valve on your water heater every three to four months to be sure the lever works properly. If the thermostat fails to operate properly, this valve will prevent a dangerous increase in water temperature and pressure.[5]

FAUCETS

To maintain proper water flow and reduce water usage, clean the aerators on faucets. An aerator adds air to the water as it leaves the faucet and eliminates splashing. It also reduces water usage, which saves money. Aerators are most common on kitchen and bathroom sink faucets. A laundry tub faucet does not have an aerator (so it can accept a hose connection). To clean an aerator, first make sure the drain is covered, then unscrew the aerator from the mouth of the faucet, make note of the order and which side was up or down, remove any deposits, remove and rinse the washers and screens, replace them in their original order, and put the aerator back on the faucet. Generally, aerators need to be cleaned every three or four months but the frequency depends on your water quality and source. If you are connected to a metropolitan water system, you probably won't need to clean them as frequently. If you are using well water, you may need to clean them more often.

🏠 TIP

Noise coming from pipes when the hot water is turned on may indicate there is air or even steam in them. Reducing the water temperature, tightening up brackets holding piping in place at and up to a fixture, and adding air cylinders at the device may alleviate the noise. Hire a contractor to fix *water hammer*.

DRAINS

Each plumbing fixture in your house, except toilets, has a drain trap. This J-, S- or U-shaped pipe is designed to provide a water barrier that prevents the airborne bacteria and odor of sewer gas from entering the house. Infrequently used fixtures (such as basement showers) should be turned on at least quarterly to replace evaporated water and ensure the barrier remains intact. Because of their shape, traps are also the source of most clogging problems.

TOILETS

If you purchased a used home rather than a new home, you should ensure that it has low-flow water-saving toilets. They conserve water and will save you money.

Never flush materials such as hair, grease, garbage, lint, diapers, or feminine products down the toilet. Bulk waste like these products not only can clog the toilet, it might block sewer lines. Sewage can back up into your home. Also, never use toilet cleaning products anywhere other than the toilet, and never mix them with other household products such as bleach or ammonia. You could create a dangerous, or even deadly, chemical reaction.

Most toilets have a water chamber, flush valve, overflow pipe, float, and ball valve. If the water chamber appears to leak, the moisture may be from condensation forming on the outside of the tank and dripping to the floor. If water leaks into the bowl through the overflow pipe, adjust the float so it is closer to the bottom of the tank. You can do this by bending the rod that holds the float. You also may need to adjust the chain on the flush handle. If it is too tight, it prevents the rubber stopper at the tank bottom from sealing. Flush the toilet. If it still leaks, you probably need to replace the inlet valve washer. A worn ball valve or dirt or rust on the ball seat will let water leak into the bowl. If the ball valve or ball seat is dirty or rusty, clean it. If the ball is worn, replace it. Sometimes it's best to call in a plumber.

If a toilet backs up:

- Shut off the water supply to toilet.
- Try clearing the blockage with a plunger or, if that doesn't work, with a snake.

WHEN TO CALL

If neither a plunger nor snake works, call a professional.

SEPTIC TANKS

Know whether your home is part of the municipal sewer system or if it uses a septic system for waste. All septic tank installations must meet local health standards. With proper care and attention, septic tanks will serve as satisfactorily as sewers. If they are not maintained, they can become a burdensome expense. When they function improperly, they are a neighborhood health menace.

If your home uses a septic system, learn the location of the septic tank and its drainage field. For best results, inspect it annually. The frequency with which a septic tank should be cleaned depends on its size, daily sewage intake, and the number of people it serves.

Unless the tank is large enough to accommodate additional wastes, the use of a garbage disposal will require the tank to be cleaned more frequently. When the total depth of scum and solids exceeds a third of the liquid depth of the tank, the solids should be removed. With ordinary use and care, the tank will probably need cleaning every two years. Your local health department may help you locate someone to perform this service.

Because warm weather promotes bacterial growth, septic tanks should be cleaned in the spring. The waste material gives off noxious odors and may contain dangerous bacteria. Therefore, it should be disposed of in a manner approved by your local health department. No chemicals are capable of reducing solids in a septic tank to the point where cleaning is unnecessary. In fact, cleansers generally should not be added to the sewage. They can kill the good bacteria needed for the system to function correctly.

LEAKS

All leaks raise your water bill. Leaking from an outside faucet can cause a damp basement. Leaking inside or outside faucets generally can be fixed by replacing the washers. Some faucets with single controls for hot and cold water have no washers. Instead they use cartridges. Although these cartridges last longer than washers, they still must be changed periodically. Many cartridges will last 20 years without maintenance, while washers might need attention in fewer than 10 depending on use and brand. Before attempting to repair a faucet, turn off the water at the nearest intake valve. Washers and cartridges are available at most hardware or plumbing supply stores.

TROUBLESHOOTING: *LEAKS*

Leak from one sink, tub, or toilet: Check the condition of caulking and grout. Is it missing entirely or peeling from the surface? Also confirm that the shower door or tub enclosure was properly closed while in use. Turn off water supply to area in question. Use an alternate bathroom and call a professional.

📞 WHEN TO CALL

For a leak in the main line, turn off the water at the meter and call for service.

PIPES

Copper pipes should last 50–100 years (fewer in areas of very hard water or wells) or close to the lifetime of a house. However, if a joint loosens or a fitting joint leaks, it will need to be resoldered—a job best left to a plumber. Plastic pipe should also last the lifetime of the house, and a loose joint likewise should be repaired by a plumber. If your washing machine, dishwasher, or other water-using appliance appears to leak, first check to see that the drain trap is completely open. Sometimes a partially clogged drain can cause an overflow.

CONSERVING WATER

- Promptly repair leaking devices indoors and out. A leaky faucet can rapidly waste gallons of water.
- Run the dishwasher only when it is full.

- Turn off the faucet while brushing your teeth or shaving.
- Take short showers rather than baths.
- Adjust the washing machine water level according to load size.
- Don't overwater plants.
- Water the lawn early in the morning (preferable) or late in the evening to reduce evaporation.
- Don't overmow. Allowing grass to grow somewhat (3"–4") provides shade for roots and improves water retention in the soil.
- Grow plants suitable for the climate zone. This can save more than 50% of the water normally used to care for outdoor plants.
- If you wash your car at home, turn the hose off between rinses.
- Cover an outdoor pool when it is not in use.

REMINDERS

Quarterly:

- Turn on infrequently used fixtures, such as basement showers
- Check around water heater for leaks. If you have hard water, drain 1 to 2 gallons of water
- Check faucets for leaks, clean aerators, and replace washers as needed.
- Clean drains with baking soda.
- Pour water down unused drains.
- Check under and around kitchen and bathroom cabinets for leaks.
- Check toilet for stability and leaks.

Annually:

- Clean septic system.
- Flush water heater.

NOTES:

Your electrical system is a three-wire grounded system. It is equipped with safety features such as circuit breakers and *ground-fault circuit interrupters (GFCIs)* that shut off the electricity and warn you of possible danger at a switch or in the system. The electrical *service entrance* provides power to the service panel. It has been designed for the electrical needs of the house. Do not tamper with this cable. Never remove the bare wire that connects to the box or device.

CIRCUIT BREAKERS AND FUSES

These devices protect the electrical wiring and equipment in your home from overloading. They are the safety valves of your home's electrical system. Breakers trip from overloads caused by plugging too many appliances into the circuit, or from a worn cord or defective appliance, starting an electric motor, or operating an appliance with a voltage requirement higher than what the circuit was designed to handle. If a circuit trips repeatedly, unplug

📞 WHEN TO CALL

If a circuit trips when nothing is connected to it, call an electrician.

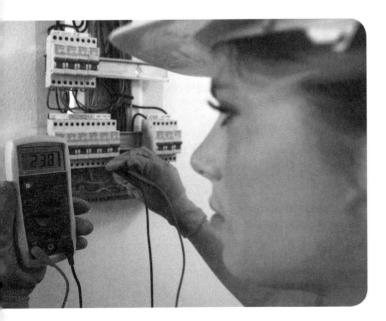

everything connected to it and reset it. If it stays on, one of the items you unplugged is defective and needs repair or replacement. If the circuit trips when nothing is connected to it, call an electrician as soon as possible.

Every house should have a master circuit breaker. It generally is located near the smaller circuit breakers. Tripping the master circuit breaker cuts off electricity to the house. Circuit breakers may be reset by first switching the breaker to full off and then back to full on.

Ordinarily, small appliances that require personal attendance while operating may be plugged into any outlet. However, operating many small appliances or one large one on a single circuit can overload it. If this happens frequently, contact a licensed electrician to discuss whether your home needs additional wiring.

GROUND-FAULT CIRCUIT INTERRUPTERS

The receptacles in your kitchen, bathrooms, and outdoors should be equipped with GFCIs. These safety devices are commonly installed where small appliances (such as hair dryers) are used near sources of water, which can "ground" a person and electrocute him or her if the appliance malfunctions or is dropped into water. GFCIs cut the flow of electricity to the appliance within a fraction of a second if they detect a change in the flow of current to (and from) the appliance. One GFCI breaker may control

❗ CAUTION

Never plug a refrigerator or freezer into a GFCI-controlled outlet. These appliances will probably trip the breaker. They might be the only devices on the breaker so you might not notice they are off and the food inside might spoil.

up to four outlets. If a breaker trips during normal use, an appliance may be at fault. You will need to investigate the problem. Test your GFCI receptacles monthly by pressing the "test" button. This will trip the circuit. To return service, press "reset."

ⓘ CAUTION

A short circuit is a fire hazard.

TROUBLESHOOTING: POWER FAILURE

In case of a complete power failure, first determine whether your neighbors have power. If they do not, notify the power company. If the power failure affects only your home, confirm the following:

- The main breaker and individual breakers are on.
- Applicable wall switch is on.
- GFCI is set.
- Item is plugged in.
- Item works in other outlets.
- Bulb in lamp is good.
- The power line to your home has not been damaged or cut.

Even if performing these tasks does not identify a solution, the information you gather will be useful to the electrical service provider. If one circuit breaker continues to trip, check to see if you have overloaded the circuit. If not, call an electrician. A short circuit is a fire hazard.[6]

APPLIANCES

Your new appliances come with instruction manuals and other papers. Read this literature carefully and fill out and mail the documents necessary to record warranties. Keep your purchase receipts and a list of authorized service agencies with each instruction manual. You can also go to the forms at **www.nahb.org/hmme** to record important information about your appliances such as their serial numbers and dates of service or repairs.

If an electrical appliance fails to operate, be sure it is plugged in before you call a repair service. If the appliance is separately wired, be sure the circuit breaker is still on (*see* Circuit Breakers and Fuses).

If a gas appliance with a standing pilot light fails to work, check to see if the pilot light is lit; many gas appliances now use electric ignitions. If you suspect a gas leak (if you smell a sulphur- or rotten-egg–like odor, for example), turn off the main gas valve near the meter and call the gas company immediately from another location.

ⓘ CAUTION

Do not light matches, smoke cigarettes, make phone calls, or turn lights on or off near a suspected leak.

REMINDERS

Check the following quarterly:

- Wiring, cords, and plugs for wear or damage
- GFCI circuits for proper operation

Exercise circuit breakers in the spring and fall.

NOTES:

7 FIREPLACES

Consider your fireplace a luxury, rather than a home-heating feature. A fire in the fireplace creates a warm and cozy atmosphere but adds little heat to a home. As little as 10% of the heat from a fire in an open masonry fireplace radiates into the house. In many older homes, the air used by the fireplace for combustion is replaced with cold outside air drawn in through cracks around doors and windows.[7]

WOOD BURNING

Your fireplace will add elegance and warmth if you use it safely and clean it frequently. You should avoid using it in extreme cold or windy weather when the chimney draft will rapidly draw air out. A wood-burning fireplace should be equipped with andirons (or a grate) and a well-fitting screen. It may have glass doors as well.

If you are in a newer home with a fresh air vent to supply the fireplace with combustion air, open it and the damper before you start a fire. Then remember to close both when you are not using the fireplace. Leaving them open is like leaving a window open. If the fire is still burning but you are finished enjoying it, close the glass doors if you have them to prevent heated air from being drawn up the chimney (until you can close the damper). But don't close glass doors over a roaring fire, especially if you are burning hardwoods like oak or hickory; the heat could break the glass. When you close the doors over a burning fire, open the mesh screens first. This prevents excessive heat buildup on the mesh, which might warp or discolor it.

ⓘ CAUTION

Don't close glass doors over a roaring fire, especially if you are burning hardwoods like oak or hickory; the heat could break the glass.

Keep the damper closed when the fireplace is not in use so warm air will not escape in the winter and cool air will not escape in the summer. Build fires on the andirons or grate — not directly on the fireplace floor. Seasoned hardwood is the best fuel. Do not burn pine logs in your fireplace; they contain tar that can start a fire in the chimney if it accumulates. Do not burn trash in the fireplace. Never use kerosene, gasoline, charcoal lighter fluid, or other highly flammable liquids to start a fire. Be sure the fire is out each night before you go to bed.

Making a Fire

You want to create a clean, steady, slow-burning fire. Begin with a small fire to allow the components of the fireplace to heat up slowly. Burn kindling and newspaper under the grate; stack two to three layers of logs with air space between them, placing the largest logs to the rear. You can burn one sheet of paper atop the stack to help the chimney start to draw.[8] Occasionally throwing a handful of salt on the fire will help prevent soot accumulation and add color to the flames, but you should never use salt in a metal fireplace.

Remove all but a light layer of the old ashes and coals from under the grate when completely cool. A light layer will act as an insulator for future fires and help reflect heat.

Store firewood outside away from the house. Wood may harbor insects that you wouldn't want in your home, and wood stored outside will burn longer and hotter if you keep it dry. You should split logs that are 6″ in diameter or larger.

WHEN TO CALL

Call a chimney cleaning professional for service at least once every 5 years (or every 2 years if you frequently use your fireplace). If you have a spark arrester, a professional should clean it also.

Cleaning

A chimney cleaning professional should periodically check and clean your chimney, at least once every five years if you hardly or never use your fireplace and more frequently if you use it a lot. The inspection can determine the condition of the cap, *flashing*, mortar, spark arrester, and caulking, and detect potential paths for water to enter your home.

If your fireplace has a spark arrester, have it professionally cleaned as necessary. If it becomes clogged, the diminished air flow will affect the performance of the fireplace and may be a fire hazard.

GAS

A gas fireplace provides the comfort and style of a wood-burning unit, but requires far less maintenance. Many gas fireplaces are also far more efficient than their wood-burning counterparts and as a result, produce less pollution. Gas fireplaces may have a chimney or may vent exhaust gases (mainly water vapor and carbon dioxide) directly outside without a chimney. Others are ventless; there is no flue.

⊘ CAUTION

The exterior vent cover for a direct-vent gas fireplace becomes extremely hot when the fireplace is operating.

If your gas fireplace is vented, the flue or vent should be closed when the fireplace is not in use. Use the same safety precautions with a gas fireplace that you would with any other gas appliance. Do not smoke while cleaning or lighting the fireplace. Follow the manufacturer's instructions for maintenance, safety, and use of your gas fireplace.

There will be a slight delay after turning the switch on before a flame ignites. Flames should ignite gently and silently. If you notice any deviation from this or any gas smell, immediately shut off the switch and report the problem to the gas company. Excessive winds can cause a downdraft and extinguish the pilot. You will need to relight the pilot before using the fireplace.

 REMINDERS

- Inspect flues in the fall and clean if needed.
- Clean fireplace every 1 to 5 years (depending on usage).

NOTES:

8 YOUR HOME'S STRUCTURE

Your home's foundation and *bearing walls* support the entire structure, including the roof designed to keep your home dry.

FOUNDATION

Your home sits on a foundation that consists of the *footing* and the foundation walls that rest on it. Foundation walls are usually made of poured concrete, masonry block, or wood framing. If you have a basement, the foundation walls also serve as the basement walls. Foundation walls are subject to a wide variety of stresses and strains. Because the base of the wall is in the ground, it maintains a fairly constant temperature. However, the top portion extends out of the ground and may be subject to extreme seasonal temperature changes. The changes cause concrete and masonry to expand and contract.

Cracks

Combinations of stresses and temperature variations may cause cracks in the basement or foundation walls. These cracks do not affect the strength of the structures and may be easily repaired if desired. Follow these steps to fill medium to large cracks:

- Roughen the edge of the crack if it is smooth. For large cracks, undercut the crack to form a V-shaped groove to a depth about equal to the width of the crack at the surface.
- Clean out all loose particles of cement, mortar, or concrete with a wire brush or a thin blade.
- Wet the crack thoroughly.
- Fill the crack with patching cement, allowing a little extra for shrinkage. Be sure the patching mixture is suitable for the job.
- Just before the cement hardens, rub it with burlap or a similar material to give it a texture similar to that of the wall. Wetting a *trowel* and using it to go over the patch for the last time will produce a smooth surface.
- Paint it to match the rest of the wall if necessary. To repair small cracks, fill them with a heavy paste of dry *cement base paint* mixed with a little water. Force the paste into the crack with a stiff-bristle brush or putty knife. To match the existing wall finish, use a colored paint to form the paste. In lieu of cement base paint, you may use a mixture of cement and fine sand (one part cement, two parts sand capable of passing through a 100-mesh screen) mixed with sufficient water to form a heavy paste. For fine or hairline cracks, work cement base paint into the crack with a short, stiff-bristle brush.

WALLS AND CEILINGS

Your house has both bearing and *nonbearing walls*. Nonbearing walls may usually be altered without fear of structural damage, but alteration of a bearing wall must be done carefully to avoid reducing its bearing capacity.

The structural lumber in your house should have been selected in sizes and grades to safely carry the load, all of which is regulated by building codes and standards.

These *framing members* may shrink but your home has been designed to settle as evenly as possible. Wood may contract or expand with weather changes. Although heat or cold won't affect it, in extremely dry conditions (i.e., winter in the northern climates) it will shrink. In more humid conditions it may expand.

All ceilings are essentially the same in structure, but they are made of a variety of materials.

Slight cracking, nail pops, or visible seams in walls and ceilings are a normal result of wood shrinkage and deflection of rafters the drywall is attached to. You can repair hairline cracks with a coat of paint, and slightly larger cracks with spackle or caulk. You can also use a hammer and punch to correct a nail pop, or a drill for screws, and then cover the area with two to three coats of spackle. Sand the surface with fine-grain (e.g., 150 grit) sandpaper and then paint (depending on the finish). You can fill indentations from sharp objects using the same process. Because paint and wallpaper fade over time and dye lots vary, touch-ups may be visible, so the best time to make repairs is when you plan to recoat an entire wall or redecorate a room.

Interior Plaster and Gypsum Wallboard

Whether the interior walls of your home are plaster or gypsum wallboard, they should last for the life of your house without undue maintenance. In some cases, normal shrinking in framing boards causes minor cracks and nail pops to appear in wallboard or plaster walls. Popped nails should not affect the strength of the wall, so don't attempt repairs until you intend to recover the entire wall. Then, fill the cracks with spackling compound (available from a paint or home supply store) and a spackling knife, smooth it out with fine sandpaper, and then cover the entire surface with paint, wallpaper, or whatever covering you decide to use. Except in very unusual conditions, cracks should not reappear. To prevent cracks that are wider than ¼″ and a few inches or longer from reopening, follow these steps:

- Apply the spackling compound.
- Cover the crack with a strip of fiberglass mesh made for this purpose.

- Cover the mesh with thin layers of spackling compound.
- *Feather* the edges well.
- Sand smooth.

Unusual abrasions may scuff or dent the surface of plaster or gypsum walls. If this occurs, fill the indentation with two or three applications of a joint compound used for drywall taping. Smudges or spots on interior stucco finish may be removed by rubbing it with a fine grade sandpaper (size 200).

ROOFS

Your roof will protect your home and keep it dry for many years with proper maintenance. Flashing seals those places where the roof abuts walls, chimneys, dormers, or valleys where two roof slopes meet. If a leak occurs, call a qualified roofer to make the repair. A qualified roofer should inspect the roof at least every three years. If you have to walk on the roof for any reason, be careful not to damage the surface or the flashing. Be particularly careful when installing a TV or radio antenna, satellite dish, solar hot water panels, or photovoltaics: a careless job can cause leaks.

 WHEN TO CALL

Have a professional check for missing shingles, and inspect flashing around roof openings such as chimneys, stacks, vents, and skylights semiannually or after severe weather. Vents and louvers also should be checked for evidence of vermin.

Freeze-Thaw Cycles

Winter storms followed by relatively mild temperatures cause freeze-thaw cycles that can start roof leaks. Most roof shingling is not a waterproof membrane. Rather, shingles are meant to shed water down their overlapping courses into gutters or off the roof overhang. Erratic weather conditions can cause a buildup of water—either from snow or *ice dams* formed on the roof or in gutters and downspouts. This water backs up under the shingles or eventually seeps through the shingles, causing leaks. Although roofs with a shallow pitch are more susceptible to this phenomenon than steeply pitched roofs are, no conventional home is completely immune to the problem. Remove ice blockades from gutters and downspouts, and attempt to remove built-up ice and snow from the lower portions of the roof. If your roof is vulnerable to ice dams (because of the home's design or orientation on the lot, for example), you can have electric gutter heater strips installed at vulnerable areas.

Severe Weather

After severe weather, visually inspect your roof for damage. Roof leaks cannot be repaired while a roof is wet, but you should call a professional to schedule the roof work for after conditions dry out.

 WHEN TO CALL

Notify your insurance company if you find pieces of shingle in the yard or if shingle edges have lifted from the roof.

TROUBLESHOOTING: *ROOF LEAK*

Confirm that water is coming from a roof leak, and not from any of the following:

- Plumbing leak
- Open window on a higher floor
- Ice dam
- Clogged gutter or downspout
- Blowing rain or snow through roof vents
- Gap in caulking

Place a container under dripping water if possible. If water is coming from a ceiling, poke a small hole in the drywall to release the water.[9]

ATTIC

The space directly below the roof can vary in size from a small storage space to an extra room.

Storage

Many homes have attic space which can be used for storage. However, the attic walls may not be insulated, so the space can be susceptible to extreme temperatures. Do not store combustible or perishable materials in attics. Do not place heavy materials in the attic. The floor (if there is one), may not be as strong as the floor in your living area.

Insulation

Do not allow materials stored in the attic to compress insulation (whether blown-in cellulose or traditional fiberglass). Occasionally, the insulation on the attic floor may be displaced, leaving gaps or blocking the path of attic ventilation. If either of these situations occurs, return the insulation to its proper location, but protect your skin, eyes, nose, and mouth if you will be handling fiberglass insulation. The attic access cover may have insulation attached to the top side. It should also remain securely in place so that less heat is lost through this entryway or hatch.

Make sure the insulation does not block air vents. The vents must remain unobstructed to prevent the buildup of condensation and to allow the proper amount of air to circulate in your attic. Insulation should not touch the underside of the roof sheathing.

 REMINDERS

- Inspect visible areas of the foundation quarterly for cracks and around vents and ducts for leaks for blockages.
- Check semiannually for deteriorating bricks and mortar, for damaged or rotting siding, and for flaking paint.
- Clean gutters and downspouts in the spring and fall, checking for leaks, misalignment, or damage.
- Inspect the attic semiannually for evidence of leaks or vermin.

9 INTERIOR WALL FINISHES AND FLOORING

Regular cleaning and maintenance keep the interior of your home looking fresh. Use the right techniques and tools for wall, floor, and ceiling surfaces. The *Home Maintenance Made Easy* forms at **www.nahb.org/hmme** help you keep track of these important details.

WALLS AND CEILINGS

The interior walls and ceilings of your new home should last for many years with proper care. Blistering or peeling paint may indicate an underlying problem. Touch up the spot immediately to prevent further damage but also investigate the cause, such as moisture penetration through overhead joints, plumbing fixtures, or finishes. Consult your home improvement store or paint and wallpaper dealer for the correct cleaning compound for painted surfaces and wallpaper. Also allow professionals to help you choose paint colors that will achieve your goals for a room.

You can record important information about the interior and exterior paint on your home in the online forms at **www.nahb.org/hmme**.

Paneling

Interior walls may be paneled in wood, cork, and myriad synthetic materials, some of which look like wood. Most of these are stain resistant and easy to clean. Wood paneling may require a special wood cleaner, but some wood for interior walls has been treated or coated so that it is as stain resistant and as easy to clean as the synthetics. Care of these varies with the materials, but usually a cloth dampened in a mild solution of detergent and water, followed by a clear water rinse, is appropriate. Check with the supplier of your paneling to learn what is best for your specific wall surface.

TRIM AND MOLDING

Trim and molding, such as baseboard quarter round, may separate from the floor and leave a small space that will catch dust and dirt. This separation is part of the normal process of settling and shrinking in your home. Loosening the quarter round or other trim and renailing it in its proper position will remedy the problem. If a small separation occurs at corners or at other seams, it can be patched with wood filler; however, sometimes further settling will bring the pieces together. The filler can be stained or painted to match the molding. A thin piece of cardboard or heavy paper slipped under the molding will protect the floor or rug while you are painting.

Use putty, filler, or latex caulk to fill minor separations at mitered joints in door trim; then paint.

FLOORING

Many environmentally friendly flooring options are available today. You can get flooring finishes with virtually no formaldehyde or *volatile organic compounds (VOCs)*.

Among today's wide variety of flooring options are the following:

- **Carpet.** Green carpeting choices include some that are manufactured from recycled plastic bottles.
- **Bamboo.** Because the plant grows to maturity in fewer than 10 years, it is considered a green flooring choice.
- **Cork.** This material also is considered a green choice because it is harvested from trees without killing them, and it grows back.
- **Tile.** This is a popular choice in kitchens, bathrooms, laundry rooms, and other potentially wet areas because of its ability to stand up to moisture.
- **Stone.** Not all stone surfaces have the same properties. Marble is much more porous than slate, for example. Therefore, you may see slate used in larger and more trafficked areas such as kitchens and marble in smaller spaces, such as a foyer, bathroom, or hearth.
- **Concrete.** This low-maintenance material is available in various colors and textures.
- **Wood.** Hardwood floors are popular for their durability and classic style.
- **Other hard surfaces.** New products mimic linoleum or vinyl but contain no polyvinyls. Some laminates mimic the appearance of wood or other natural materials.

Although flooring options continue to expand, following are some guidelines for caring for some popular types.

Carpet

Most carpet has built-in stain resistance which prevents spills and dirt from settling in the fibers. But although most stain-resistant treatment is fairly effective, it is not a substitute for prompt cleanup of household mishaps. Attaching rests to the bottom of furniture legs distributes weight better and helps protect carpet. Periodically rearranging your furniture can help your carpet wear more evenly by changing where the high-traffic areas are and where heavy furniture may crush carpet

fibers. Your carpet should require little maintenance beyond regular vacuuming (two light and one *thorough vacuumings* a week) and occasional cleaning for tough stains or buildup of dirt in high-traffic areas. Vacuuming high-traffic areas daily will help keep the carpet *nap* upright. A *light vacuuming* is three passes. A thorough job is up to seven passes. Purchase a vacuum with a *beater bar* for more effective cleaning.

The following substances will permanently stain even stain-resistant carpet:

- Hair dye
- Shoe polish
- Paint
- Ink

 TIP

High humidity may cause carpet to ripple. If the ripples remain after reducing the humidity, have a professional restretch the carpeting using a *power stretcher*, not a *knee-kicker*. Maintaining optimal humidity helps control static electricity buildup, which increases with cooler temperatures.

The following substances will destroy or change the carpet color:

- Bleach
- Acne medication
- Drain cleaner
- Plant food
- Insecticides
- Some food or beverages such as mustard or herbal teas with natural dyes

Keeping interior doors closed forces air (and the particles it contains) under the gap below the doors and into the carpet. Over time a noticeable stain will develop at the threshold. If you plan to use carpet stain removal products from a supermarket or home supply store, read the manufacturer's instructions carefully before using. You may want to apply a small amount of cleaner to an out-of-view area of the carpet to test for color fading. Have your carpet professionally cleaned once a year.

The following practices can delay color fading:

- Frequent vacuuming
- Regularly changing HVAC system filters
- Preventing high humidity
- Reducing sun exposure[10]

Hardwood

Hardwood floors are precisely manufactured and should be expertly installed and finished by skilled crafts-people. Regular vacuuming or dry mopping will remove surface dust and dirt. Gritty sand is wood flooring's worst enemy. Use protective mats at exterior doors to keep sand and grit off of floors. If your floors have a polyurethane finish, you should vacuum them regularly and wipe them occasionally with a damp (not wet) mop or cloth. You can use a mixture of 1 cup vinegar to 1 gallon of warm water. Do not use water on hardwood floors finished with anything other than polyurethane. Water sometimes will raise the wood's grain and prolonged moisture may cause cracks from the wood expanding and shrinking.

Hardwood floors with other finishes probably will need periodic waxing; how frequently depends on the amount of traffic they receive. Always use either a liquid or paste spirit wax. The wax can be buffed most easily with an electric polisher, which you probably can rent from a hardware or grocery store. If you use a "self-polishing" liquid wax, make sure it was made for use on hardwood floors. On moderately soiled floors where traffic is not excessive, cleaning and polishing can be done in one operation with clean-and-wax products. To use these, remove black marks with dry steel wool, sweep or dry mop to remove loose dirt, and apply the clean-and-wax product according to the manufacturer's directions. Rinse the applicator in water to remove any soil. If floors become excessively soiled, they can be cleaned with mineral spirits or household clean-ers that leave a protective coat of wax as they clean. Keep cleaners and waxes away from baseboards; these areas don't receive much foot traffic to soil them so you will be able to minimize wax buildup and not have to remove the wax as often.

As with carpet, attach furniture rests to the bottom of furniture legs resting on wood flooring to protect floors and distribute weight. Placing heavy furniture or dropping heavy or sharp objects on hardwood floors can make them dimple. High heels can exert more than 8,000 *psi* of pressure on a floor. If heels have lost their protective cap, they will mar the floor.

 TIP

Attach glides/felt pads to furniture legs to protect flooring.

Bamboo

Treat bamboo flooring as you would other prefinished wood floors. Regularly vacuum, use a dry dust mop, or sweep to remove sand, dirt, and grit. You may use a damp—never wet—mop occasionally. You can sand and refinish the floor as needed as with any solid or engineered wood flooring.[11]

Cork

Use a spirit wax or wax cleaner. Minor stains can be sanded with fine-grade sandpaper. Re-wax after sanding the stain. Cork floors may need two coats of wax with a buffing after each. Epoxy-coated cork floors are stain resistant.

Tile

Ceramic tile normally needs only vacuuming to stay clean and look like new. You can also mop the floor with a solution of ¼ cup to ½ cup baking soda or dishwasher crystals per gallon of water. Abrasive cleaners will dull the finish. If necessary, a more thorough cleaning with a detergent or ceramic tile cleaner will remove grime.

Although tile will resist stains, the grout may not. Use a fiber brush and a mild cleanser to clean yellowed or stained grout. You can have the grout sealed to help it resist stains but you will need to maintain the seal. Tile will separate from the grout. This is not a structural issue by itself; grout does not hold the tile in place. You can fill gaps using premixed grout available at flooring, hardware, and home improvement stores. You must maintain both the grout and caulking to prevent water damage to the underlying surface.

Laminate

Follow the manufacturer's instructions for removing stains or minor scratches. For routine cleaning, sweeping or vacuuming with a brush is generally all that's required. For occasional mopping, use a solution of ¼ cup vinegar per gallon of water. If you use a spray bottle to wet and mop one small area at a time, you can avoid streaking. A microfiber cloth or disposable mopping wipe works well. Moisture can damage laminate flooring so wipe up liquid spills immediately.[12]

Resilient

Asphalt, linoleum, rubber, and vinyl are examples of resilient floors. For daily care, remove loose dirt with a broom, dust mop, or vacuum. Wipe up spills immediately, but if a spill or spot dries, remove it with a damp sponge, cloth, or mop. Rubber-backed floor mats will often yellow vinyl and linoleum. To prolong the period between cleanings, occasionally wipe resilient floors with a damp mop. Excessive water on resilient floors can penetrate seams and get under the flooring material, causing it to lift and curl, so limit the amount of water you use when mopping.

Resilient floors can tear and wrinkle when you move appliances across them, so install coasters to prevent damage. If a nail head appears in the flooring, place a block of wood over it and hit the block with a hammer to reset the nail.

When floors are dull or cannot be refurbished by mopping, clean them thoroughly with a household floor cleaner recommended by the floor manufacturer. Use just enough mechanical action with a mop, cloth, or floor scrubber to loosen dirt. Remove the cleaning solution, rinse the floor, and let it dry. Some resilient floors are designed to never need waxing, but some require a coat of floor polish.

Although your flooring contractor can discuss how to care for your particular floor, the best polish for most resilient floors is water emulsion wax. Apply either the wax or a floor finish to a clean, dry floor. These finishes provide hard films that do not smear; however, they also do not respond to buffing. Waxy polishes leave softer films with slightly lower gloss that can be buffed to restore a shiny appearance. Apply these polishes sparingly, using the least amount that can be applied without streaking; allow the floor to dry for about 30 minutes before walking on it. Some porous floors may require two coats with a buffing after each one. Remove built-up polish or wax about once a year. Dilute the removal agent as recommended, apply, rinse, allow to dry, and apply a new coat of polish.

📞 WHEN TO CALL

If you aren't sure about how to care for your floor, call a professional.

Marble

As with many other hard surfaces, marble is damaged by abrasions from dirt, sand, and grit. Remove dirt with a brush attachment on the vacuum (taking care not to scratch the surface with the wheels of the vacuum cleaner) or use a dry, untreated dust mop. Blot spills with a paper towel (don't spread them by wiping). Use a mild dishwashing liquid and water, and rinse several times.[13] Never use vinegar or any other acidic product to clean marble: it will etch the marble. Household bathroom cleaners will do likewise. Check with your fabricator or installer about how to safely clean your marble floor.

Slate

Slate is less porous than marble but to make it easier to maintain, it can be sealed. Then, for regular cleaning you can mix a mild detergent, such as laundry detergent, with water for mopping. Rinse thoroughly with plain water and dry the surface with a cloth that won't shed or catch on the rough surface.

Concrete

Concrete floors generally don't require maintenance other than cleaning by sweeping or vacuuming. A stiff brush will help to loosen dirt. A concrete sealer will make an unpainted concrete floor easier to keep clean. Follow the manufacturer's directions for cleaning after the sealer has been applied. Never use soap on unpainted concrete. Instead, use a solution of 4–6 tablespoons of washing soda to a gallon of water (if necessary, use scouring powder with the washing soda solution). First, wet the floor with clear water. After cleaning, rinse the floor with clear water. Painted concrete floors can be cleaned with plain water or a mild soap or detergent solution. Concrete floors may crack under some conditions. Read more about repairing cracks in chapter 8, Your Home's Structure, and chapter 12, Exterior. Occasionally basement floors will collect condensation moisture.

You can record details about your floor, including how to care for it and room square footage (for when it's time to replace your flooring) using the forms available at **www.nahb.org/hmme**.

REMINDER

Inspect tiled areas quarterly for loose or missing grout or caulk and repair as needed.

The doors and windows that adorn your home contribute to its curb appeal and provide daylighting. But they also can be a major source of air leakage that compromises your insulating system, makes a space uncomfortable, and raises heating and air-conditioning costs.

WEATHER STRIPPING

To maintain your home's energy efficiency, exterior doors come equipped with weather stripping made from a variety of materials, such as metal, plastic, or rubber. This weather stripping must remain in place to prevent the loss of expensively conditioned air or infiltration of outside air. Metal weather stripping may need to be renailed if it becomes loose, bends away from the edge of the door, or does not seal tightly when the door is closed. This simple repair requires only a pair of pliers to hold the tiny nails and bend the metal to fit the door, and a hammer and the right size and type of nails. For rubber or plastic weather stripping, renailing or regluing with a strong, water-resistant household glue should be all that is necessary. Do not use a cyanoacrylic ("super") glue.

STORM DOORS

A storm door may reduce your heating costs. Storm doors are usually made of aluminum, wood, vinyl-clad wood, or solid vinyl. Homes with insulated steel exterior doors do not need separate storm doors. Even in mild climates, where they are less prevalent, storm doors can help reduce heating and air-conditioning costs and provide an added security barrier.

MAINTAINING AND FIXING DOORS

Doors provide security and, when chosen and installed correctly, can save money on heating and cooling. You can correct simple door problems yourself; you don't need to call in a professional.

Painting and Cleaning

Wood exterior doors should be painted on the same schedule as the house and trim—about every 4–6 years. Stained exterior doors should be sealed with a varnish or polyurethane. You can add a coat of finish every three years after a light sanding and touching up where stain might have been gouged or scratched.

Aluminum, vinyl-clad wood, and solid vinyl doors do not need to be painted. Steel and fiberglass doors come preprimed, but they need to be finished with at least 2 coats of good quality latex paint on the front and back and around the edges. As always, follow manufacturers' instructions.

Sticking

This is the most common problem with doors. Do not plane a door that sticks during a damp season. Wait to see if it continues to stick after the weather changes. If it does, apply paste wax, paraffin, or candle wax to the sticking surface; or tighten the screws that hold the door jamb or door frame before resorting to planing. To plane, fold sandpaper around a wooden block and sand the door edge that sticks, and then paint. Paint and varnish protect wood from moisture and help to prevent further door problems.

Warping

Slight warping, also usually caused by excessive moisture, may be corrected by keeping the door closed as much as possible. If that doesn't work, you can dry it in the sun. If the door is still warped after being thoroughly dried, apply weights to the bulged side and leave them in place for two to three days.

GARAGE DOORS

Lubricate the moving parts of garage doors (tracks, rollers, hinges, pulleys, and springs) every three months with silicone spray. Check that all hardware is tight and operates as intended, without binding or scraping. Avoid using too much lubricant, which can drip on vehicles or the concrete floor.

Tighten the screws that fasten the hardware to a wood door every 12 months because the wood shrinks a little as it ages, so the screws may loosen. If a hinged wooden door sags, tightening or adding *turnbuckles* should bring it back into shape. Each garage door usually requires two of these, one on each of two cables crisscrossing the back of the door. An overhead door may warp inward if left up for long periods. Usually this warp can be corrected by adjusting the nuts on the metal rods or the straps across the top and bottom of the door. It is important to replace bent or cracked panels on wooden doors to prevent other panels in the door from warping.

Metal garage doors require less maintenance, but you will still need to tighten the screws and grease the track and trolley.

Sliding garage doors that drag can be realigned by tightening the bolts on the wheels that run on the overhead track. Also, make sure the floor guide is not out of alignment.

Repaint the garage door when you repaint your home, or more often as needed. A professional should repair garage door springs.

WINDOWS

Your windows may be framed in a wide variety of materials, including aluminum, steel, wood, solid vinyl, and vinyl-clad wood. Wooden frames should be painted whenever the house or house trim is painted (every 4–6 years). Aluminum, vinyl, and vinyl-clad wood do not need painting. Steel frames should be painted with rust-inhibiting paint. Aluminum can be allowed to oxidize (it will turn gray). This protects it from the elements; however, if you prefer to maintain the bright look, you can apply a coat of wax. This is easier than polishing aluminum that has already oxidized, but you can polish it with steel wool.

Storm Windows

Many houses in temperate climates do not need storm windows. If your house has dual-glazed windows (two layers of sealed glass with a space for air or another gas between them), you may not need storm windows. In extreme climates, storm windows over insulated glass may be cost-effective for energy conservation. Using storm windows will reduce your heating and cooling bills. Be sure to clean both the glass and the screens when you exchange them in the spring and fall.

Skylights

A skylight may leak if its seal breaks around the plastic or glass opening. The contractor who replaces your roof should weave new shingles into the existing skylight flashing system and ensure the roof drains from the top layer of shingles. When your roof is being inspected for general maintenance, have the seals, caulking, and flashings around skylights inspected for any cracks or interruptions. A quality flashed skylight doesn't need tar for water tightness, so don't just add tar and hope, call in a professional.

☎ WHEN TO CALL

Call a professional to fix a leaking skylight. It may not have been flashed properly.

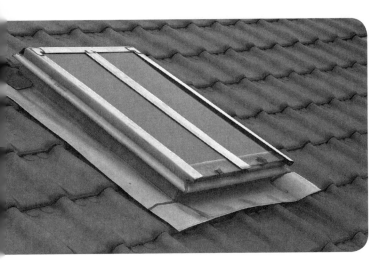

Cleaning

If the outside of a window is extremely dirty, use a piece of crumpled newspaper to wash the glass with a solution of equal parts vinegar and water (lightly soiled windows will usually respond to a solution of 1 cup vinegar to 1 gallon of water) or 3 tablespoons of denatured alcohol per quart of warm water. You may also use a household glass cleaner. Apply the cleaning solution with a sponge or lintless cloth and dry the glass with a chamois or lintless cloth, and/or squeegee. The window frames can be cleaned with a mild detergent solution. Marble sills require special care. Marble care is discussed in chapter 11, Kitchens and Baths.

Minor Repairs

If a window does not slide easily, rubbing the channel with a piece of paraffin or a bar of soap should help. An old candle will do. The same treatment will work for sliding wooden closet doors. For metal doors and windows, use a silicone lubricant. Never use oil: it will collect dirt and eventually make sliding more difficult.

Wood windows may need new glazing compound occasionally. Remove cracked, loose, or dried-up glazing compound, and clean out dust and dirt with a clean, dry brush. Replace any missing glazier's points (the small pieces of metal that hold the glass in place). Roll some fresh glazing compound between your hands to stretch it out. Fit it against the glass and the wood with your fingers and smooth it with a putty knife. Oil paint can be mixed with the compound to color it, or it can be painted.

For a broken window, remove the remaining glass, all old glazing compound, and glazier's points. For a broken window that is not framed in wood, consult a supplier for advice on replacement.

🗓 REMINDERS

- Check weather stripping and caulking around windows and doors, and exchange screens and storm windows, in the spring and fall.
- Lubricate the moving parts of garage doors quarterly and tighten screws connecting hardware to wooden doors annually.
- Clean window and door tracks, and *weep holes*, and lubricate rollers and latches quarterly.
- Clean exterior of windows annually.

KITCHENS AND BATHS

Kitchens and bathrooms have been transformed from utilitarian rooms into luxurious spaces with special features and dramatic finishes. You can preserve and prolong their beauty with regular maintenance and cleaning.

KITCHENS

Kitchens have a variety of finishes: tile, slate, vinyl, wood, stainless steel, enamel, glass, and others. To keep your kitchen looking fresh, use the cleaner and protector appropriate for each finish.

Cabinets

Clean wood cabinets as you would any fine wood furniture. Ask the manufacturer what cleaners to use on your cabinets. You can use lemon oil or polishes that include scratch cover on wood cabinets. Use these products only every 3 to 6 months to avoid buildup. Don't wipe cabinets with the same rag you use on dishes or for wiping dirty countertops. Also, don't use appliances that generate moisture (coffeemakers, Crock-Pots) under or near a cabinet. The moisture can warp and discolor cabinets. Keep a screwdriver or other appropriate tool handy in the kitchen to quickly tighten hinges to align cabinet doors and secure handles and knobs that may work loose. You can use silicone lubricant sparingly to help hinges and drawer glides operate smoothly.

Countertops

Countertops are generally heat- and stain-resistant with normal use, but they should be protected from hot pots, pans, or baking dishes taken from an oven or stove top. Do not cut food directly on the countertop because the knife may dent or nick the surface. Countertops made of plastic-coated wood or metal may be cleaned with a detergent solution. Nonporous countertops resist stains. If a solid-surface countertop stains, you may be able to rub the stain off using a soft cleanser or fine sandpaper.

TIP

Cutting food on countertops can leave scratches and nicks. The finish is then susceptible to stains, which become increasingly difficult to remove.

Because marble is easily stained or etched, you should protect it according to the manufacturer's instructions. Compatible sealing, polishing, and cleaning products are available from marble suppliers and from some hardware stores.

Granite and solid-surface materials do not stain easily and are less prone to scratching than marble. These countertops require occasional polishing.

Unfinished wood countertops or work surfaces made from unfinished wood require special care. To protect them from spills, coat the surface (including the edges) lightly with olive oil, let the oil soak in for a few minutes, and rub dry with a soft lint-free cloth. Several thin coats will provide better protection than one heavy coat.

To remove odors caused by onion, garlic, and other foods, rub the wood surface with a slice of lemon, sprinkle lightly with salt, and immediately wipe with a soft cloth or paper towel. Clean unfinished wood countertops

FOOD STAINS

Most food stains can be removed with a mild chlorine bleach solution (3 tablespoons per 1 quart water), but check with the material manufacturer to ensure this won't damage the surface. For stubborn stains, wait five minutes before rinsing. An alternative for stubborn stains is a paste of equal parts cream of tartar, 6% hydrogen peroxide, and a household cleaner. Leave paste on the stain for 10–15 minutes before rinsing.

with a mild bleach solution once a week, rinse thoroughly, and wipe dry. If you do not have a built-in chopping block, buy portable cutting boards to protect your countertops. Always use a dedicated board to cut raw meat.

Caulk

The caulk between the countertop and the wall, along the joint at the backsplash, and around the sink may shrink, leaving a slight gap. Maintaining a good seal in these locations is important to keep moisture from reaching the wood under the laminates and to prevent warping.

Sinks

Sinks are generally made of porcelain enamel or stainless steel. A blow from a heavy or sharp object will chip porcelain enamel. Scraping or banging metal utensils will gradually scratch and dull the surface of any sink. Abrasive cleaners and steel wool pads will damage the finish of a stainless steel sink. Use either a nonabrasive cleaner or one made specifically for stainless steel.

Prolonged contact with bleach can pit sink surfaces. Prolonged contact with produce can stain them. Your water also affects the appearance of your stainless steel sink. Overly softened water or water with a high concentration of minerals can develop a white film on the sink. Hard water can cause a brown surface stain that looks like rust.

 TIPS

- Laundry tubs or sinks are usually made of fiberglass or plastic and should require only cleaning with a nonabrasive cleanser.
- Wet metal utensils left on the surface of the sink or tubs can cause rust stains. Steel wool soap pads also will rust and stain when wet and should be kept in an appropriate container. Rust stains are almost always permanent on fiberglass surfaces.

To keep all sinks looking fresh and clean, do not let food waste stand in them. Use your disposal or throw the waste in the garbage can. Do not use sinks to hold paint cans, trash, or tools when you are redecorating. Cover fixtures when painting walls, ceilings, and woodwork. If a paint splatter on porcelain enamel dries before you wipe it up, use a recommended solvent to remove it.

Garbage Disposals

If you have a garbage disposal, the manufacturer's instructions will give precise directions for disposal operation. Always use cold water when the disposal is on and especially when grinding greasy substances. Many people mistakenly conclude that because their waste disposal is capable of grinding up most food waste, it is also capable of eliminating grease and other substances they would not otherwise pour down a drain. In fact, you should be equally careful not to clog disposal drains with grease. In addition, avoid putting fibrous materials such as banana peels or corn husks, or large bones, in your disposal. If the disposal and drain clog, do not pour in chemicals.

Reset Button

Most disposals have a reset button that works like a circuit breaker. (See your appliance's instruction booklet.) If the disposal becomes overloaded with something it cannot grind, it will automatically turn off. If this happens, turn the switch off, remove the offending substance, wait about three minutes, and push the reset button. Switch the garbage disposal on; if it still doesn't start, turn the switch off and check to see whether you have tripped the circuit breaker. If the circuit breaker has been tripped, turn off the circuit breaker (as a safety precaution) and use a mop or broom handle to turn the rotating plate in the disposal unit until it turns freely. Then restore current, push the reset button again, and turn the disposal switch on.

Some disposals come equipped with a special wrench or tool that can be inserted either in a hole in the bottom of the disposal (under the sink) or into the top of the rotating plate. Turning the wrench a couple of times should loosen the material enough to get the disposal to start.

ⓘ CAUTION

Be absolutely sure the circuit breaker is off before inserting a broomstick, wrench, or anything else to remove material when the disposal is stalled.

BATHROOMS

It's much easier to keep your bathroom clean and stain-free by regularly wiping its surfaces than to try to remove with harsh chemicals stains and water deposits that have been allowed to set.

Bathtubs, Sinks, and Showers

Bathtubs, sinks, and showers comprise various materials. Bathtubs are most frequently made of vitreous china, porcelain enamel on cast iron or steel, or fiberglass-reinforced plastic. Bathroom sinks are usually made of vitreous china, of porcelain enamel on cast iron or steel, or marble resin. Showers are most frequently made of ceramic tile, fiberglass, reinforced plastic, or molded plastic.

Bathtubs and sinks can retain their luster for many years. However, once they are damaged, even the best refinisher cannot make them look new. To prolong the life of bathtubs and sinks, follow these precautions:

- Never wear shoes in a bathtub. Gritty shoe soles can scratch the surface, regardless of the material.
- Do not use strong abrasive cleansers. Although most household cleaners are mildly abrasive, they are safe to use with plenty of water. But to ensure you don't scratch surfaces, use a nonabrasive cleaner. Baking soda is not abrasive.

Glass Shower Enclosures or Stalls

Remove water with a squeegee or wipe after every shower. You can also use wax or lemon oil **(not on the floor!)** to prevent mineral and soap film residue buildup. Use dishwashing detergent to clean. If hard water minerals have built up, use a cleaner recommended for the surface.

Jetted Tubs

Follow the manufacturer's directions for use and care. Never operate the jets unless the water level is at least 1" above the jets. Clean and disinfect the system every 1–2 months as follows:

- Fill tub with lukewarm water and 1 cup of liquid chlorine bleach.
- Run jets for 10–15 minutes.
- Drain and refill the tub with just water.
- Run jets for 10 minutes.
- Drain tub.

Marble and Manufactured Marble

These surfaces will not chip as easily as porcelain enamel but a sharp blow, abrasive cleansers, water that is too hot, and razor blades can damage manufactured marble. Always mix hot and cold water at manufactured marble sinks.

Fixtures

Avoid using abrasive cleaners on gold or antique brass fixtures. Use mild detergent and water or a cleaning product the manufacturer recommends. When peeling, spotting, or discoloration occurs, you can sometimes restore the beauty of the metal by completely removing the remaining coating and hand-polishing the item with a suitable brass polish. Applying a light coat of wax and buffing with a soft cloth helps maintain the gloss. Like silver, brass will gradually tarnish; an antique appearance is normal.

CAULK

When the caulk around your bathtub or sink dries out or cracks, remove the old caulk and replace it. If you don't have a caulking gun, you can buy caulk in applicator tubes or in disposable caulking guns from a home supply store. Fill the tub with water before caulking it. Use a smooth motion and apply the caulk in a small bead (it will spread as you *tool* it). Use a damp finger, cloth, or caulk tool available at home centers, to flare the edges back to the surrounding surfaces and work the caulk into joints. You can use painter's tape on the adjoining surfaces to achieve a clean, straight line. Silicone caulk is a good choice for areas that must cope with excessive of moisture. It is more difficult to clean and tool, and you have to be quicker, but you will have to caulk far less frequently.

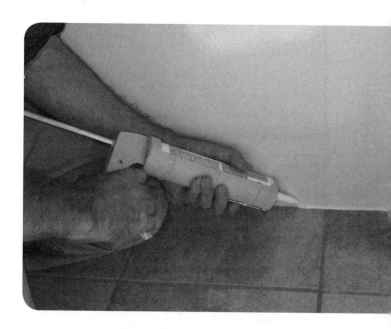

NOTES:

EXERIOR 12

Your home's exterior protects the interior from weather, including water damage. It also reveals something about the personality that's behind the windows and doors. Home buyers (and your neighbors) rightly judge a book by its cover. When you keep your home's exterior clean, painted, and in good repair, passersby will assume you care for and maintain the inside as well.

BRICK WALLS

Small surface chips or cracks and slight variations in size and placement are normal and help to create the texture and beauty of brickwork. Mortared joints will weather. If your home is several years old, the brick may require *tuck pointing* (repairing the mortar between the bricks).

 WHEN TO CALL

Have a professional mason apply new mortar as needed to keep the exterior weather resistant.

Do not fill or allow landscaping to cover weep holes in the brick. These holes allow moisture to escape from the brick, which is a porous material. You can clean glazed tile or bricks with soap and water. For stubborn discoloration, gently scrub with a nonabrasive household cleaner or a special tile cleaner. Clay masonry homes may require cleaning by a specialist who may use steam or a steam-and-water jet with a cleaning compound.

 TIP

A white powdery substance composed of one or more crystallized soluble salts sometimes develops on masonry walls. This is called efflorescence. It is a natural phenomenon that you cannot prevent. However, in some cases you can remove it with a stiff brush dipped in vinegar. Your hardware or home improvement store may have commercial products to remove it.

SIDING

Wood, vinyl, and cement board plank or shingle-style are among the many types of exterior siding available.

Wood

If your home has wood siding, you should not have to worry about wear. Where paint is thin, cracked, or peeling, the siding should be scraped, sanded, and repainted to prevent moisture penetration and rot. Do not overpaint the exterior of your home because excessive repainting builds up an unnecessary and troublesome thickness of paint, which may crack and peel. Siding made of coated plywood or plastic-finished wood may be guaranteed for the life of the house.

Aluminum, Steel, Vinyl, and Other

Many synthetic sidings are guaranteed against cracking, chipping, peeling, and termites for 10 years or longer. Most of them resist marring and scarring and are nearly maintenance free. You can easily remove dirt and fingerprints around doors and windows with a mild detergent solution. For other areas, occasional hosing may be sufficient. Any area you clean with more than a hose will have a different appearance than surrounding areas that are not cleaned, so you will need to feather the area or make a break at a wall, window, or other obstruction.

GUTTERS AND DOWNSPOUTS

Always keep gutters and downspouts clear of leaves, tree limbs, or anything that could cause overflowing. Ideally, they should be cleaned twice a year—in the spring to check how they fared in the winter, after seeds and other debris have fallen, and in the fall after most leaves have fallen. Be sure that downspouts direct water away from the foundation. Vinyl gutters never need paint. Paint is optional for aluminum gutters. Gutters made of most other metals will need a coat of rust-retardant paint

whenever the rest of the house is painted (every 4–6 years). You can seal against drips at a gutter joint using commercial gutter caulking compound.

OUTDOOR FAUCETS

If you don't have frost-proof fittings on outside water connections and the temperature falls below freezing where you live, you should turn off the water and drain pipes before cold weather sets in. This precaution will prevent the outside pipes and fittings from freezing and bursting. The control valve is usually inside the house close to where the water supply goes through the exterior wall. Open the outside faucet to drain excess water. Also disconnect the garden hose(s) and store during cold weather.

🛇 CAUTION

Water in a hose can freeze and expand back into the pipe, causing a water line break.

TERMITES

Termites are easier to bar from a new house than to exterminate from an old one. You should conduct your own inspection every spring.

- Look for remains of the winged insects.
- Search the sides of basement or foundation walls and piers for the earthen tubes that termites build to reach the wood above the foundation.
- Tap wood to see if it sounds or feels hollow.

- Inspect under the carpet tack strip by lifting the edge of carpet in the corner of a room. (The tack strip is untreated and provides a convenient path for termites through your home.)
- Use a knife blade to test wood for soundness.
- If you suspect termites, consult a professional exterminator.

 **WHEN TO CALL.** Call a professional exterminator if you notice signs of termites.

HARDSCAPING

Various materials are used for driveways, walks, steps, patios, and decks. Concrete and asphalt are most common for driveways. Walks and steps are usually concrete, but they may be made of brick or other material.

Concrete

Avoid washing exterior concrete slabs with cold water from an outside faucet in hot weather and when sun has been shining on the concrete. The abrupt temperature change can damage the surface bond of the concrete. Also protect concrete from chemical agents such as pet urine, fertilizers, radiator overflow, repeated hosing, or de-icing agents such as road salt. These substances can cause *spalling*. Remove ice and snow as quickly as possible and do not allow heavy commercial vehicles on your driveway, which is probably designed only to be used by conventional residential vehicles such as cars, vans, and light trucks.

> **SUMP PUMP**
>
> Your foundation design may include a perimeter drain and sump pump. The pump may run continuously during heavy or prolonged rain. Make sure you keep the sump pump discharge clear of debris and that you have a backup power source for the pump in case of an electrical outage during a storm. Periodically confirm that the pump is plugged in, the circuit breaker is on, and the pump operates. To see whether it operates, pour five gallons of water into the sump pump *crock* (hole). The pump should pump the water out.[14]

Contraction and expansion joints in concrete work help minimize cracking. However, cracking is a characteristic of concrete. Severe frost can sometimes cause cracking. You can repair minor cracks as follows:

- Roughen the edges of the crack if they are smooth.
- Clean out loose material and dirt.
- Soak the old concrete thoroughly. The crack should be sopping wet, but water should not be standing in it.
- Fill the crack with patching cement slightly higher than the crack to allow for shrinkage. Commercially prepared patching mixtures need only the addition of water, but be sure the mixture you buy is appropriate for concrete.
- Cover the patch and keep it damp for several days. The longer the drying time, the stronger the patch will be.
- When the cement has partly set, remove excess cement with a wire brush. At this stage the surface of the cement appears sandy.

Deck

Although the wood used to build decks is usually *pressure treated*, you still generally need to perform some maintenance on it to protect it from moisture. If a floor board warps you can screw it back down or replace it. You should preserve your deck by applying a water repellant or wood preservative periodically.

FENCES AND RAILINGS

Fences and railings are decorative elements as well as safety features. To keep them attractive and in good repair, don't allow sprinklers to spray them. Cracking, warping, and splitting are normal for wood. As the wood ages and shrinks, you may need to reset nails. Also check posts and gates twice a year and adjust hardware.

Inspect wrought iron twice a year and touch up scratches or chips as needed with paint to prevent rust. Repaint the entire surface every one to two years.

> ### 📅 REMINDERS
>
> - Check foundation quarterly and exterior walls semiannually, repairing bricks, mortar, siding, and paint as needed.
> - Disconnect garden hoses and store before the first frost.
> - Check for evidence of termites in the spring.
> - Clean and check gutters and downspouts in the spring and fall.
> - Clean concrete and asphalt of oil and grease quarterly and check for needed repairs semiannually.
> - Clean your deck and apply a protectant in the spring.

13 LANDSCAPING

A good landscaping plan increases the beauty and value of your home and can save money on heating and cooling: strategically placed trees and shrubs can shade your home in summer and shield it from chilling winds in the winter. Aesthetically, consider the landscaping around your house as an extension of the indoor living space. Plan it with a long-term view, envisioning how you want it to look in 10 years. The grounds should include defined areas for relaxation, gardening, entertaining, and play, which you can screen or partition using trees, shrubs, and other greenery.

Sketch the areas you want to reserve for turf, and precisely locate each shrub and tree where you want to plant it. Consider each plant's space requirement at maturity, particularly if you expect to plant young stock. If all of this sounds like a lot of work, remember that a thoughtful plan minimizes wasted effort in the long run. Adhere to the plan, making changes only if they improve the overall scheme.

Color, size, shape, texture, and blooming seasons are all important considerations in choosing plants. You will need taller shrubs for privacy, trees for shade, flowering trees for color, low-growing plants under windows, and thicker evergreens in the background.

The beauty of having a landscape plan is that you can execute it gradually or more rapidly, depending on how much time and money you have. To start the design, use graph paper to make a scaled sketch of your property. Plot your home, driveway, walkways, porch, patio and/or deck, trees, fences or walls, and other features. Indicate where doors and windows are; they influence your plan too: you don't want to provide hiding places for people who might be up to no good, but you also want to be able to see beautiful foliage from your windows and shade your home during hot weather.

GRADING

Drainage *swales* or other discharge channels were sized and sloped to accommodate water runoff and should be kept clear of debris such as leaves, gravel, and trash. Do not alter the grading pattern with landscaping. Allow 6″ between your grading and the wall siding. Otherwise, water may enter the joint between the foundation and the wall material, or the wood may decay. Compacting soil may cause depressions. Fill these with soil so water will not pool.

🏠 TIP

Do not place plantings or sprinkler heads within 5' of your home.

CARING FOR NEW GRASS AND SHRUBS

If you are in a new home, water the lawn and shrubs often. In the fall of the first year, rake the lawn thoroughly, reseed it, and add organic fertilizer or manure. Pay special attention to bare spots. When watering the lawn, help prolong the paint on your home by avoiding sprinkling it. If you plant flower beds near the house, do not disturb the earth next to the foundation. Always dig the beds several feet away.

NATIVE PLANTS

Find out which trees and shrubs grow well in your region. Make a list of plants that appeal to you. Then research how to grow and care for them. Decide what to plant, where, and how much money you will need to budget.

Because native plants have adapted to local conditions, they are more resistant to pests. You can use non-persistent pesticides, which break down into harmless components, before sowing native plant seeds. Once native plants are established, pesticides are seldom needed. Also, when you use native plants for landscaping, you minimize the need for gasoline-powered lawn and garden equipment. This equipment produces, on average, 5% of ozone-forming VOCs in areas with smog problems and emits toxins and particulates.

 TIP

> The National Gardening Association has a handy "Plant Finder" resource at **http://www.garden.org/plantfinder/**. Your local garden club (find yours at **http://www.gardenclub.org/clubs/state-clubs.aspx**), nursery, or cooperative extension service (locate yours at **http://www.csrees.usda.gov/Extension/**) are also good resources.

Benefits of Native Landscaping

Native landscaping benefits the environment. When planted in the soils and conditions to which they have adapted, native plants require less water, fertilizer, and labor. Native plants provide the following benefits:

- Filtering pollutants and controlling storm water runoff. Many native plants have very deep root systems so they can prevent flooding and erosion.
- Providing appropriate food and shelter for native wildlife.
- Preserving genetic, botanic, and biological diversity.
- Reducing the need for pesticides.
- Improving air quality.

> **MAINTAINING YOUR NATIVE LANDSCAPE**
> - Pull weeds monthly (or more frequently) if needed.
> - Water plants during periods of extended drought.
> - Control undesirable/invasive plants.

Place mulch at least 3" deep to retain moisture, discourage weeds, and prevent soil compaction. Do not allow edging around decorative rock or bark beds to dam the free flow of water away from your home. You can use a nonwoven landscape fabric between the soil and rock or bark to restrict weed growth while still allowing normal evaporation of ground moisture.

Prepare clay soils before planting. For grass, Rototill (parallel to swales) 2" of sand and 1" of treated, odorless manure into soil to a depth of 6". These steps will help your lawn retain moisture and require less watering. Here are some other tips for water- and energy-efficient landscaping:

- Use deciduous trees to provide shade during the summer and permit solar warming in winter.
- Plant evergreen trees and shrubs to create a windbreak and reduce heating costs.

- Position trees to shade the roof and still allow good air flow around the home.
- Plant shrubs and trees to shade the air conditioner without obstructing air flow around the unit.
- Group together plants with similar water, sun, and space requirements.

 REMINDERS

- Check the drainage around your home quarterly.
- Prune, rake, and mulch in the spring or fall as appropriate.

NOTES:

_____

_____

_____

_____

_____

_____

_____

_____

_____

_____

_____

_____

_____

_____

_____

_____

_____

_____

APPENDIX

MISCELLANEOUS HOUSEHOLD TOOLS AND SUPPLIES

Tool Kit—You will need a few basic tools and supplies for everyday use in keeping your home in top shape. A suggested list follows:

- Medium-sized adjustable wrench
- Standard hand pliers
- Needle-nose pliers with wirecutter
- Screwdrivers—small, medium, and large with standard and Phillips heads
- Electric screwdriver
- Claw hammer
- Rubber mallet
- Hand saw
- Assorted nails, brads, screws, nuts, bolts, and washers
- Level
- Plane
- Small electric drill
- Caulking gun
- Putty knife
- Tape measure

Other tools can be rented or purchased as needed.

Fire Extinguisher—Every home owner should buy at least one fire extinguisher. Each member of the family should be familiar with its location and operation. Have it checked annually to be sure it functions properly and is fully charged. Be sure you and your family know how to turn off the electricity, gas, and water in the event of an emergency. Keep in mind that fires from combustible solids such as wood, cloth, or paper, and electrical and chemical fires, are very different. Each type of fire calls for a different type of fire extinguisher. Most home supply centers sell multipurpose fire extinguishers which can be used for most types of small fires. Read more about fire extinguishers and fire safety in chapter 1, Safety and Security.

First Aid Kit—Keep a home first aid kit or first aid materials in a convenient location. Buy and keep with them a booklet on first aid and home safety.

Duplicate Keys—Have duplicate keys made and keep them in convenient places so small children who lock themselves in the bathroom or other rooms can be freed promptly. When you take a vacation, leave a key with a trusted neighbor. If you forget to attend to something before you leave or if an emergency arises, your neighbor might be able to take care of it.

SAFETY INSPECTION

(Your local fire department may perform this service at no charge)

- Check storage areas, backs of closets, basement corners, and other out-of-the-way places, and properly dispose of fire hazards such as oily rags, unvented gas cans, painting supplies, and flammable cleaning materials.
- Check stairs, steps, and ladders for problems that could cause a fall or other accident. Check handrails and railings.
- Check all connections to your electrical system to correct any possible hazards. Replace frayed electrical cords and do not overload extension cords.
- Keep driveways, walks, and steps free of ice and snow to avoid damage to them and to prevent hazardous walking and driving conditions.

HOME MAINTENANCE SCHEDULE

Depending on where you live, most of the items on this schedule will apply to your home. You can also find it online at **www.nahb.org/hmme**.

MONTHLY

		DATES COMPLETED		
Carbon monoxide detector	Test for proper operation and replace batteries if necessary			
Heating and cooling systems	Clean or replace filters according to manufacturer's recommended schedule.			
Lights	Test lights in infrequently used spaces to be sure they will work when they are needed.			
Security	Test each sensor and the primary and backup batteries.			

QUARTERLY

DATES COMPLETED

Plumbing

Drains	Clean with baking soda. Pour water down unused drains.			
Faucets and shower heads	Check interior and exterior faucets for leaks. Clean aerators. Replace washers if necessary.			
Kitchen and bathroom cabinets	Check under and around for leaks.			
Pipes	Inspect visible pipes for leaks.			
Toilets	Check for stability and leaks.			
Water heater	Check area around water heater for leaks. If you have hard water, drain 1-2 gallons water.			

Interior

Basement or crawl space	Check for cracks or any sign of dampness or leaks. Check for any evidence of termites or wood-eating insects.			
Ceramic tile	Check and clean grout.			
Garage door	Lubricate hardware. Inspect mechanism for free travel.			
Interior doors	Lubricate hinges.			
Window and door tracks	Check to see if weep holes are open. Clean out dirt and dust. Lubricate rollers and latches.			
Wood cabinets and trim	Apply a wood protectant.			

Electrical and appliances

Dishwasher	Check for leaks. Clean and replace filters according to manufacturer recommendations.			
GFCI outlets	Test for proper operation.			
Kitchen exhaust fan	Remove and clean the filter. Clean accumulated grease deposits from the fan housing.			
Refrigerator	Clean dust from top. Clean refrigerator drain pan. Clean and defrost freezer if necessary.			
Smoke detector	Test for proper operation and replace batteries if necessary.			
Wiring, electrical cords, and plugs	Check for wear or damage. Replace if necessary.			

Exterior

Concrete and asphalt	Clean oil and grease.			
Foundation	Check for proper drainage.			
Landscaping	Inspect visible areas, vents, and ducts for cracks, leaks, or blockages.			

FALL   DATES COMPLETED

Plumbing

Faucet aerators	Check for proper flow of water. If the flow is reduced, clean the aerator screens. During the first two months, the faucet aerators could require more frequent cleaning.			
Outside faucets	Drain.			
Plumbing shut-off valves	Inspect for proper operation.			
Water heater	Flush out hot water to remove accumulated sediment.			

Interior

Attic	Examine for evidence of any leaks. Check insulation and remove or add if necessary. Check for evidence of birds, squirrels, raccoons, etc. Check for proper ventilation.			
Countertops	Inspect for separations at sinks and backsplash. Recaulk where required.			
Fireplace	Inspect flues. Clean if necessary. Inspect fireplace brick and mortar for cracks or damage.			

Sectional garage doors	Adjust the travel and tension.			
Shower doors/tub enclosures	Inspect for proper fit. Adjust if necessary. Inspect caulking and recaulk if necessary.			
Smoke, carbon monoxide, radon detectors	Test and clean units with a vacuum or cotton swab, clean filters as applicable, and replace batteries and lightbulbs.			
Tiled areas	Inspect for loose or missing grout or caulking. Regrout or recaulk if necessary.			
Weather stripping	Check caulking around windows and doors.			
Windows	Exchange screens for storm windows as needed.			

Electrical and appliances

Cooling system	Remove debris from around units and clean with garden hose. Remove window air conditioner or protect with weatherproof cover. Clean and replace filters if necessary.			
Combustible appliances	Inspect and service if necessary.			
Heating system	Service heating system and heat pump.			
Refrigerator	Clean coils.			

Exterior

Chimney	Clean and check for deteriorating bricks and mortar. Check for leaks. Check for birds, nests, squirrels, and insects.			
Concrete and asphalt	Check for cracks or deterioration. Reseal or repair if necessary.			
Exterior walls	Check for deteriorating bricks and mortar. Check siding for damage or rot. Check painted surfaces for flaking.			
Gutters and downspouts	Clean and check for leaks, misalignment, or damage.			
Hoses	Remove and store before first frost.			
Landscaping	Remove tree limbs, branches, or debris that can attract insects. Trim shubbery around walls. No wood or branches should be closer than 3" from your house. Maintain grading. Rake leaves. Mulch.			
Lawn and patio furniture	Clean and store or cover with weatherproof material.			
Roof	Check for leaks. Check for damaged, loose, or missing shingles. Check vents and louvers for birds, nests, squirrels, and insects. Check flashing around roof stacks, vents, and skylights for leaks.			
Septic system	Examine septic system drain field for flooding and odor.			

Plumbing

Water heater	Flush out hot water to remove accumulated sediment.			

Interior

Attic	Examine for evidence of leaks. Check insulation and remove or add if necessary. Check for evidence of birds, squirrels, raccoons, etc. Check for proper ventilation.			
Countertops	Inspect for separations at sinks and backsplash. Recaulk where required.			
Shower doors/tub enclosures	Inspect for proper fit. Adjust if necessary. Inspect caulking and recaulk if necessary.			
Smoke, carbon monoxide, radon detectors	Test and clean units with a vacuum or cotton swab, clean filters as applicable, and replace batteries and lightbulbs.			
Tiled areas	Inspect for loose or missing grout or caulking. Regrout or recaulk if necessary.			
Weather stripping	Inspect all doors and windows for proper operation and a tight fit. Check caulking around windows and doors and replace as needed. Exchange storm windows for screens as needed.			

Electrical and appliances

Circuit breakers	Exercise.			
Heating and cooling system	General furnace inspection: Look for rust, scaling on heat exchanger, and proper flame color; note odd sounds or smells; and check condition of venting. Remove debris around units.			
Refrigerator	Clean coils.			

Exterior

Chimney	Clean and check for deteriorating bricks and mortar. Check for leaks. Check for birds, nests, squirrels, and insects.			
Concrete and asphalt	Check for cracks or deterioration. Reseal or repair if necessary.			
Decks	Scrub mildewed areas and treat for water stains, mildew, and fungus.			
Exterior walls	Check for deteriorating bricks and mortar. Check siding for damage or rot. Check painted surfaces for flaking.			
Gutters and downspouts	Clean and check for leaks, misalignment, or damage.			

Landscaping	Remove tree limbs, branches, or debris that can attract insects. Trim shubbery around walls. No wood or branches should be closer than 3" from your house. Maintain grading. Rake leaves. Mulch.			
Roof	Clean. Check for leaks. Check for damaged, loose or missing shingles. Check vents and louvers for birds, nests, squirrels, and insects. Check flashing around roof stacks, vents, and skylights for leaks.			
Septic system	Clean.			
Termites	Check for evidence of.			
Windows	Clean.			

ANNUALLY DATES COMPLETED

Plumbing

Septic system	Have tank pumped.			
Sump pump	Check operation.			

Interior

Fire extinguisher	Check to ensure the charge is in the green area of the scale.			
HVAC	Have a professional clean and, if necessary, repair your system before using it the first time of the season (fall for heating and spring for air-conditioning).			
Paint	Survey condition and repaint as needed.			

Exterior

Landscaping	Seed and feed lawn (spring or fall). Prune and divide perennials (spring, summer, and/or fall, as appropriate).			

EVERY 1 TO 5 YEARS DATES COMPLETED

Interior

Bathroom/laundry exhaust fans	Clean. (Frequency depends the type of fan.) Check for dust and lint that accumulate around dampers, blades, and grille.			
Fireplace	Clean. (Frequency depends on usage.)			

OWNER'S MAINTENANCE RECORD

This list can also be found online at **www.nahb.org/hmme**.

INTERIOR	DATES CHECKED			REMARKS
Appliances				
Electrical cords and plugs				
Fire extinguisher				
Ranges, ovens, broilers—controls, thermostats, timers, surfaces, heating elements, pilots, and valves				
Security systems				
Smoke alarms				
Washer and dryer—vents and connections				
Attic				
Electrical wiring				
Inside roof sheathing				
Insulation				
Louvers and vents				
Basement				
Flooring				
Insulation				
Masonry joints and surfaces				
Stairs				
Baths, Sinks, and Showers (see also "Plumbing")				
Caulking				
Grouting				
Surfaces				

Electrical

Circuit breakers				
Fixtures				
Lightbulbs				
Outlets and switches				
Service entrance				

Fireplace

Ash collector				
Chimney or flue				
Damper				
Flashings				
Mortar joints				

Heating and Air-Conditioning

Air registers and returns				
Blower fan*				
Burners*				
Ducts and dampers				
Filters				
Flue or chimney*				
Gas line*				
Humidifier				
Motor*				

*May be part of an annual professional inspection.

Heating and Air-Conditioning (*cont.*)

Pilot*				
Refrigerant*				
Thermostat				

Plumbing

Aerators				
Drains				
Faucets				
Pipe connections				

Surfaces (Check for cleaning, refinishing, and repairing)

Ceilings				
Floors				
Trim and molding				
Walls				

Water Heater

Mineral deposits				
Pressure relief valve				
Temperature setting				

Windows and Doors

Caulking				
Hinges, handles, locks				
Painted surfaces				

*May be part of an annual professional inspection.

INTERIOR   DATES CHECKED   REMARKS

Windows and Doors (*cont.*)

Sashes				
Thresholds				
Tracks and rollers				
Weather stripping				

EXTERIOR   DATES CHECKED   REMARKS

Foundation

Check foundations of deck, porches, and patio				
Drainage				
Masonry joints and surfaces (Check for cracks and termites)				

Grounds and Miscellaneous

Address identification				
Drains and splash blocks				
Driveway				
Exterior lights and outlets				
Grades				
Mailbox				
Lawn				
Recreation equipment				
Septic tank				
Sidewalks and steps				
Trees, shrubs, and other plantings				

Grounds and Miscellaneous (*cont.*)

Utility entrances and meters				
Walls, fences, gates				

Roof

Antenna mounts				
Chimney				
Flashing				
Gutters and downspouts				
Roofing				
Vents				

Surfaces (Check for cleaning, refinishing, and repairing)

Masonry				
Siding				
Trim and Molding				

Windows and Doors

Caulking				
Glazing				
Screens				
Shutters				
Storm windows and doors				
Skylights				
Weather stripping				

SUPPLIERS AND CONTRACTORS

Store *Home Maintenance Made Easy* and all of the instruction manuals and manufactures' warranties received with your new home in a convenient place so that the information will be easy to locate if needed. List the names and telephone numbers of your suppliers and contractors below.

ITEM	NAME	CONTACT INFORMATION
Air cleaner		
Air-conditioning		
Brick		
Cabinet		
Ceramic tile		
Concrete or cement		
Dishwasher		
Disposal		
Driveway		
Drywall		
Electrician		
Garage doors		
Gutters and downspouts		
Heating system		
Insulation		
Landscaping		
Masonry		
Microwave oven		
Millwork (doors, windows, trim, etc.)		
Painting		

ITEM	NAME	CONTACT INFORMATION
Plaster		
Plumbing and fixtures		
Range, oven, broiler		
Refrigerator		
Resilient flooring		
Roofing		
Security system		
Siding		
Sliding glass doors		
Trash compactor		
Washer and dryer		
Water heater		
Weather stripping		
Wood flooring		

WARRANTY NOTES

ITEM	SERIAL #	MODEL #	LENGTH OF WARRANTY	SERVICE PROVIDER
Appliances				
Clothes dryer				
Clothes washer				
Dishwasher				
Freezer				
Garbage disposal				
Ice maker				
Microwave				
Oven and hood				
Refrigerator				
Range, stove, or cooktop				
Trash compactor				
Heating and ventilation				
Air-conditioning				
Boiler				
Electronic air cleaner				
Exhaust fan				
Furnace				
Heat pump				
Humidifier				
Space heater				
Thermostat				

ITEM	SERIAL #	MODEL #	LENGTH OF WARRANTY	SERVICE PROVIDER
Mechanical and/or Electrical				
Burglar alarm				
Carbon monoxide detector				
Central vacuum system				
Doorbell				
Electric meter				
Fire alarm				
Fire extinguisher				
Garage door opener				
Gas meter				
Gas or electric barbecue grill				
Intercom				
Radon detector				
Smoke detector				
Water meter				
Water pump				
Plumbing				
Sump pump				
Water heater				
Water softener				

FLOORING NOTES

ROOM	SQ. FT.	COLOR/STYLE	STORE/INSTALLER	CARE/CLEANING

PAINT NOTES

ROOM	# OF GALLONS	COLOR	FINISH	STORE PURCHASED

CHECKLIST FOR EXTENDED ABSENCE[15]

- ☐ Hire someone to mow the lawn or shovel snow.
- ☐ Alert police or your community's security company when you will be away.
- ☐ Stop mail, newspapers, and other deliveries.
- ☐ Use lighting timers.
- ☐ Confirm that property insurance policies are current and provide sufficient coverage.
- ☐ Mark valuable items with identifying information. Consider whether you have irreplaceable items that should be stored in a bank vault or security box.
- ☐ If you have a landline, forward phone calls to a relative or close friend.
- ☐ Unplug computers and other electronic devices that might be harmed in an electrical storm.
- ☐ Leave window coverings in their most typical positions.
- ☐ Confirm that all doors and windows are locked and the deadbolts are engaged.
- ☐ Shut off the main water supply and open faucets to relieve pressure in the lines.
- ☐ Set the thermostat on the water heater to "vacation" to save energy.
- ☐ Leave the water heater (filled with water) on and set to the lowest setting, or empty it and turn it off as follows: Shut off the cold water supply valve on top and the gas control at the bottom. Drain the tank by running a hose from the spigot on the bottom of the heater into a drain.
- ☐ Store items such as your lawn mower, bicycles, or ladders in the garage or otherwise out of sight.
- ☐ Disengage the garage door opener (pull on the rope that hangs from the mechanism). Use the manufacturer's lock to bolt the overhead door. Caution: Attempting to operate the garage door opener when the manufacturer's lock is bolted will burn out the motor of your opener. When you return, unlock the garage door first, then re-engage the motor (simply push the button to operate the opener and it will reconnect) to restore normal operation.
- ☐ Leave a car in the drive.
- ☐ Summer: Turn your air conditioner fan to "on." Set the thermostat to 78°F.
- ☐ Winter: Set the thermostat to at least 55° F. Leave doors on cabinets that contain plumbing lines open. Leave room doors open. These steps allow heat to circulate.
- ☐ Arm your security system, if applicable.

AGING IN PLACE AUDIT

Check any of the following items that present problems and consult a professional remodeler for assistance. A professional remodeler can make adjustments to your home to improve your quality of life as you age.

Entry
- ☐ Climbing up the stairs to the front door
- ☐ Going down the stairs from the front door
- ☐ Unlocking the front door
- ☐ Using the doorknob
- ☐ Reaching and using the mailbox
- ☐ Walking over the lip at the threshold
- ☐ Seeing in the area

Hallways and Inside Doors
- ☐ Opening and going through doors to rooms
- ☐ Using door knobs
- ☐ Moving between carpeted and non-carpeted areas
- ☐ Seeing because of inadequate lighting
- ☐ Turning on lights in the area being approached

Stairs
- ☐ Slipping on stairs
- ☐ Distinguishing thresholds and edges
- ☐ Tracking over bare treads or other obstacles
- ☐ Balancing support

Kitchen
- ☐ Turning lights on and off
- ☐ Using electrical outlets
- ☐ Opening and closing windows
- ☐ Seeing because of inadequate lighting
- ☐ Using cabinets, closets, or other storage
- ☐ Using and reaching all parts of the refrigerator/freezer
- ☐ Using counters or other surfaces (preparing meals)
- ☐ Using the oven (door, dials, shelves)
- ☐ Reaching the switch on the range fan
- ☐ Using the stove (dials, reaching burners)
- ☐ Opening cans or bottles
- ☐ Using water taps
- ☐ Cleaning the floor and other surfaces
- ☐ Using the dishwasher
- ☐ Disposing trash/garbage

Bathroom
- ☐ Entering and exiting
- ☐ Privacy
- ☐ Turning lights on and off
- ☐ Using electrical outlets
- ☐ Using cabinets and closets
- ☐ Using the mirror
- ☐ Using water taps
- ☐ Using the sink
- ☐ Using the toilet
- ☐ Using the shower/bathtub
- ☐ Opening and closing the window

Bedroom
- ☐ Entering and exiting
- ☐ Privacy
- ☐ Turning lights on and off
- ☐ Using electrical outlets
- ☐ Communication
- ☐ Opening and closing drapes, shades, and/or curtains
- ☐ Opening and closing windows
- ☐ Using the closet (opening/ closing, reaching clothes)
- ☐ Finding adequate storage room
- ☐ Tripping on rug corners and edges
- ☐ Seeing because of glare
- ☐ Seeing because of inadequate lighting

Living Room or Family Room
- ☐ Entering the living room
- ☐ Turning lights on and off
- ☐ Using electrical outlets
- ☐ Glare from the outdoors or from lights
- ☐ Seeing because of inadequate light
- ☐ Opening and closing drapes, shades, and/or curtains
- ☐ Opening and closing windows
- ☐ Moving around in the living room
- ☐ Monitoring the heating and cooling system
- ☐ Tripping on rug corners and edges
- ☐ Entertaining guests

NOTES

[1] Carol Smith, *Homeowner Manual: A Template for Home Builders, Second Edition,* Washington, DC: Home Builder Press, 2001.

[2–10] Ibid.

[11] Build it Green™ fact sheet, "Bamboo Flooring," revised June 10, 2005, http://www.builditgreen.org/attachments/wysiwyg/22/Bamboo-Flooring.pdf, accessed Oct. 1, 2012.

[12] "Cleaning Laminate Flooring," http://www.woodlaminateflooring.org/cleaning-laminate-flooring.php, Accessed Sept. 28, 2012, WoodLaminateFlooring.org, Copyright ©2006-2012, All Rights Reserved

[13] "Get to Know Your Stone," Marble Institute of America, http://www.marble-institute.com/consumers/care.cfm, accessed Sept. 28, 2012.

[14] Smith, *Homeowner Manual.*

[15] Ibid.

GLOSSARY

beater bar. On a vacuum cleaner, the rotating cylinder with bristles that helps lift and remove dust and dirt from your carpet.

bearing wall. A wall that helps distribute the weight load of a home. It is essential to a home's structural integrity so it should never be altered without consulting your local building code and a structural engineer.

building envelope. The foundation, roof, and walls that enclose a home.

cement base paint. A powder that includes portland cement, lime, and other ingredients in addition to pigment

combustion air. Air required for the proper operation and venting of fuel-fired appliances, such as gas furnaces, and fireplaces.

compact fluorescent light (CFL). A smaller version of a full-size fluorescent light. It saves energy because it generates more lumens per watt, generates less heat, and lasts longer than an incandescent bulb.

compressor. A machine that squeezes the refrigerant in an air-conditioning unit

condensation. The transformation of moisture in warm air to liquid water when the air meets a relatively colder surface

crock. The container from which a sump pump draws water, which sits in a pit

effluorescence. White powder that appears on the surface of masonry walls, usually caused by moisture reacting with the soluble salts in concrete.

effective age. The condition and appearance of a home, rather than how long ago it was constructed. Major system (roof, HVAC) replacements and remodeling can make an older home function and appear to be newer than it actually is.

evaporative cooler. A device that cools air by passing it through water or a wet material

feather. To reduce the thickness of an edge, as when touching up paint on a previously coated surface or when overlapping adjoining areas of paint.

flashing. Weatherproofing material used to channel water and prevent it from entering a home

flue. The opening for a chimney to convey smoke outdoors

footing. The base of a foundation that distributes a structure's load to the soil below

framing member. A structural component, such as a stud, plate, or joist, to which other building components are attached.

green home. A home designed and constructed to conserve natural resources, such as water and energy

ground-fault circuit interrupter (GFCI). An electrical outlet designed with faster overcurrent protection than a typical receptacle. It is typically installed at potentially wet locations like kitchens and bathrooms.

handler. The unit that includes heating and cooling elements, filters, and the other parts that condition the air that will circulate through a home's HVAC system.

heat pump. A device used in both heating and cooling a home that works by extracting heat from the air

hot water baseboard heating. A system that heats air using a system of pipes and panels within a room

hydronic system. A system that uses water to heat a home, cool it, or do both.

ice dam. An obstruction that can occur when snow and ice melt and then freeze

knee kicker. A tool used to make small stretches while laying carpet

light vacuuming. Making 3 passes with a vacuum cleaner over the same area

nap. The surface pile of carpet

nonbearing wall. A wall that was not designed or constructed to carry the structural load of a home

oil canning. Waving or buckling of metal ductwork that causes a loud noise

ozone. An unstable form of oxygen with practical uses but which can be poisonous at high levels

passive solar heating. A system that uses structural elements, rather than mechanical equipment, to heat a home

power stretcher. A tool used to stretch areas of carpet that are too large for a knee kicker to handle

pressure treated. A type of wood infused with chemicals, using pressure, to make it flame- and decay-resistant

psi. Pounds per square inch

radiant. A system that heats a home by heating a surface that then discharges heat into the surrounding space

register. An opening from a heating or air-conditioning duct that includes a grille and damper for adjusting airflow

relative humidity. The percentage of moisture in the air

return. In a heating or cooling system, an opening to a duct that channels air from an interior space back to the heating or cooling unit

service entrance. The point where electricity enters your home from the power source spark arrester

spalling. Chipping

spark arrester. The mesh grill on a chimney top

swale. A shallow depression

tool. To compress and shape, as with mortar

thorough vacuuming. Passing a vacuum cleaner up to 7 times over the same area

trowel. A hand tool for applying, shaping, and smoothing a substance, such as mortar.

tuck point. To finish or repair the mortar joints between bricks or stones with a narrow ridge of material

turnbuckle. A link with screw threads at each end that is used to tighten a rod or stay

volatile organic compound (VOC). A harmful chemical containing carbon that readily evaporates into the surrounding air at room temperature

water hammer. A hammering or stuttering sound in a pipeline that sometimes accompanies a sudden and significant change in the flow rate of fluid through the pipes

weep hole. A hole designed to drain water

INDEX

NAHB BUILDERS AND REMODELERS

When you purchase a new home or commission a remodeling project constructed by a member of the National Association of Home Builders (NAHB),* you benefit from the latest building research and technology as well as professional experience and expertise. Builders and remodelers who belong to NAHB and your local home builders association (HBA) have access to the latest and best developments in residential and light construction. Many are designated graduate builders and remodelers and master builders, and may be certified professionals in green construction technology and remodeling for aging in place.

*NAHB produces the annual NAHB International Builders' Show for professionals in the light construction industry and advocates for consumers by promoting policies that encourage homeownership.